Historiography

N. Jayapalan

ATLANTIC
PUBLISHERS & DISTRIBUTORS (P) LTD

Published by

ATLANTIC

PUBLISHERS & DISTRIBUTORS (P) LTD

7/22, Ansari Road, Darya Ganj, New Delhi-110002
Phones : +91-11-40775252, 40775214, 23273880, 23275880
Fax: +91-11-23285873
Web: www.atlanticbooks.com
E-mail: orders@atlanticbooks.com

Printed & bound in India by Atlantic Print Services

Preface

The present book 'Historiography' is quite comprehensive and covers all aspects. This book covers the entire syllabus prescribed by various universities. I have narrated all aspects of Historiography from the beginning to the end. I have also made a serious attempt to present the matter in a simple and lucid manner.

It is to be admitted that there is no scarcity of books on the subject Historiography. Usually specialists in this field have attempted writing, yet many of them are not free from subjectivity that is centred on sectional interest and limited perspective. Because of this, it has been found essential to present a book which is balanced, objective and comprehensive.

By and large the book is intended to serve the needs of scholars attending the institutions of higher learning. In addition, it has been designed to meet the requirements of the examinees of Civil Services Examination in History. I hope that the present book will prove to be more useful to the students than any other book on the subject available in the market.

M/s Atlantic Publishers and Distributors, New Delhi, undertook both the printing and publication of the book. I convey my thanks to them for executing the job with due care and consideration for its perfection. I also express my thanks to them for bringing this book out expeditiously and efficiently.

Suggestions, if any, for the improvement of the book in the subsequent editions will be highly appreciated.

N. JAYAPALAN

Contents

1

Meaning of History

Generally definition limits and enlightens the scope of the subject. It sets its boundaries and distinguishes it from other disciplines. In the case of history many definitions have been given by many scholars and men of letters. Although there are numerous definitions of history, the ultimate definition of history is yet to be arrived. Perhaps can never be.

The Greeks were the pioneers in defining history. The origin of the word "history" can be traced back to the Greek word 'istoria' meaning 'inquiry' or research or 'knowledge obtained as a result of inquiry'. From the Greeks the Romans came to know the meaning of history. It was then transmitted to the other world languages and assumed greater importance.

In the middle of the 5th century B.C., Herodotus 'The father of History' wrote his monumental work on the wars between the Greeks and the Persians. He called it the "Histories of Herodotus". By this he meant simply the results of his inquiries or researches into the events of the Graeco-Persian war and the events leading upto it.

Dionysius of Halicarnassus was one of the earliest to speak of the essential function of History. He said "History is Philosophy drawn from examples". Of course, by 'example' he meant real ones from life.

Sir Walter Raleigh, many centuries later, echoed the above sentiment and said "the end and scope of all History is to teach us by example of times past such wisdom as may guide our desires and action".

Aristotle, the great Greek Philosopher has defined history as "an account of the unchanging past". He went to the extent of even saying that "even God cannot change the past".

Francis Bacon said that "history is a discipline which makes men wise". History according to him produces a sobriety. This he calls wisdom. Thus he differentiates wisdom from mere intellectual alertness.

Hegel, the German Philosopher and Gibbon, the English historian have, given a pessimistic definition of history. Hegel has estimated history thus, "what experience and history teach is this — that people and Governments never have learnt anything from History; acted on principles deducted from it". This is a thought provoking view of history. If so, there would not have been a First world war followed by the Second World War which had set a great holocaust which the mankind would never obliterate from its living memory.

R.W. Emerson says that, "there is properly no history but only biography".

Thomas Carlyle also agrees with Emerson's definition of history. He declared, "as I take it, universal history, the history of what man has accomplished in this world, is at bottom the history of the great men who have worked here; social life of the aggregate of all the individual men's lives who constitute society; History is the essence of those innumerable biographies". Really speaking this definition is a narrow and restricted one. History does not stop with its dealing with men's biographies alone. As a matter of fact, it deals with the political, economic and social life of human beings.

Some historians invested history with a moral quality, *e.g.*, Lecky said, "History is the record and explanation of moral revolution".

Leibnitz echoed the above sentiment and declared that, "a History is the true demonstration of religion".

J.B. Bury made a controversial definition of History. According to him, "History is a science, no less and no more". If history means inquiry, of search and science means finding out things, then Bury's statement is a correct description of history.

According to Croce, "all history is contemporary history". Croce said this because he felt that past events became history only when they are contemplated by the historians and so history materialises only in the historians thought. "Thus all history has to be contemporary history".

Sir John Seeley is of the opinion that "history is past politics". "But this is a half truth and like all half-truths dangerous since it deludes". One cannot easily distinguish between past and present. In short politics and history are inseparable.

The great philosopher Karl Marx advocated the materialistic interpretation of history. He defined history in the following words: "The history of all hitherto existing society is the history of class struggles".

A.L. Rowse said, "History is essentially the record of the life of men in societies in their geographical and their physical environment; and said again, "the history of every country is that of the civilisation to which it belongs".

Lord Acton, the great Professor of Modern History at Cambridge, characteristically defined history as "the unfolding story of human freedom".

Seignobos interpreted history as a science. "History was essentially a science of reasoning since all historical knowledge is indirect".

In his monumental work, "The Idea of History" R.G. Collingwood, the British historical philosopher says, "the philosophy of history is concerned neither with the past by itself, nor with historian's thought about it by itself, but with the two things in their mutual relations. Following on this M. Gakeshott said, "history is the historians experience".

Voltaire said "history is just the portrayal of crimes and misfortunes".

Gibbon who was greatly influenced by Voltaire made a similar statement: he said, "History is indeed little more than the register of the crimes, follies and misfortunes of mankind".

G. Kitson Clark in his "The Critical Historian" defines history thus: History is the record of what has happened in the past, of anything that has ever happened in the past however long ago or however recently".

Allan Nevin, the American historian says that, "History is actually a bridge connecting the past with the present, and pointing the road to the future".

E.H. Carr in his work "What is History" says that, "history is a continuous process of interaction between the historian and his facts, an unending dialogue between the present and the past".

According to Henry Ford, an American businessman "History is Bank".

Moreover Burckhardt, Charles Firth, James Joyce, Sir Robert Walpole and Edmund Burke have given their useful definitions on history in their works.

From the above definitions it is very clear that history is mainly concerned with the activities of human beings. It is the study of events in man's struggle for progress. Change is the part and parcel of history as 'change is the law of life'. Therefore, a real historian is the one who would be attaching great importance to the changes that take place in political, economic, social and religious aspects of life.

To put it in a nutshell history means only a true account of what really happened in the past as well as a faithful account of such happenings.

2

Scope of History

NATURE OF HISTORY: There are certain permanent characteristics for nature of History which make it unique, and also certain transient features which may change from time to time. The nature of history will change according to the prevailing philosophy of history and even from historian to historian according to his predilection and training.

(1) As for the permanent characteristics of history, like every other discipline it has its own immutable features. History can be distinguished from science on the one hand and metaphysics on the other, literature on the one hand and fine arts like music on the other.

(2) History is man's attempt to describe and interpret the past.

(3) It is man as a rational animal and as a social animal that ultimately forms the subject matter of history.

(4) History is concerned with the lives and doings of consequential persons, the consequences being social. These 'consequences' are also known as 'importance' in history.

(5) History is secular. It is concerned with temporal, mundane matters and not with spiritual efforts.

(6) Another important characteristic feature of history is to be interested in the past.

(7) History is social memory; this is the memory of the collectivity. But it may not always be dependable.

(8) History obliges people to think and be responsible.

(9) It is very obvious that 'chronology and geography are the two eyes of history'. Chronology stands for time and geography for space. The time space continuum provides the temporal base for History.

(10) History should be concerned not generally with the past but only with the realities of the past.

(11) Another chief characteristic of history is that history repeats itself.

(12) History cannot be static as it moves in time.

(13) Croce and Collingwood have opined that history does not exist outside the historian's mind.

(14) According to Trevelyan there are three distinct functions of history *viz.*, the scientific, the imaginative and the literary.

Scope of History

The scope of history has been variously viewed by historians. Dr. K.M. Munshi defines the scope of history thus: 'The central purpose of a history, must, therefore be to investigate and unfold the values which age after age have inspired the inhabitants of a country to develop their collective will and to express it through the manifold activities of their life".

In the early days, history was considered to be nothing but a store — house of legends, heroic accounts and folk-tales. But as days passed by, the scope of history underwent significant changes.

Necessarily history has to exclude from its purview, the study of natural objects and animals, birds, reptiles etc., since it confines its attention to the story of man's evolution from humble beginnings to complex achievements.

The Arabs used to say, "History for kings and warriors, poetry for men and arithmetic for the shop-keeper". But history is supposed to give a complete picture of everything that has influenced man directly or indirectly.

In short, strictly speaking, history centres round the people inhabiting a country. It is the record of their life coming from a series of centuries, their fortunes, achievements and pitfalls.

The scope of history is to enquire into the origins of the past and to determine relationship and comparisons. It will try to discover the shapes and contours of the forces which are dynamic in society. He knows that "social forces are human energies which 'originating in individual motivations' coalesce into a collective manifestation of power" and is interested in discovering source of these powers.

Generally, it is believed that history is concerned with man's past achievements, whether the idea or the event in question occurred one minute ago or a thousand years ago. The past is of different kinds. It looks good for some people; and for others it is incredible. Some are proud about the past and talk about golden ages. Some scholars assume that history had a very good start but by the time it reached the hands of a historian for treatment it gets deteriorated. Others are more hopeful and suppose that the historical process resembles the growth of a person from innocent childhood to knowledgeable and mature adulthood. In spite of his occasional pitfalls and repressions man has been generally progressing.

In this connection it is better and fitter to explain the dictum that 'one man's flesh is another man's poison'. A history that had been euologised by its admirers for its signal and significant service having done to humanity as a whole, now came in for severe criticism at the hands of historians like Voltaire and Gibbon. So they began to say that, "history is just the portrayal of crimes and misfortunes". Equally Gibbon retorted by saying that, "History is indeed little more than the register of the crimes, follies and misfortunes". Moreover the wide horizon of knowledge includes man's achievements in his scientific, technological, political, economic, social and cultural spheres of life in which he has mastered. Thus the main scope of history will be the social life of man, his diurnal achievements, his constitutional arrangements and his economic endeavours. Indeed they intimately affect the welfare of man in his day to day life.

In shaping the destiny of the world many great men rendered remarkable services. History never failed to include their names. This takes us to the 'Greatmen Theory' in history. Thomas Carlyle was the great exponent of this theory. He believed that, "the universal history at its bottom was the work of greatmen". Lord Buddha, Alexander the Great, Akbar the Great, Abraham Lincoln and Napoleon Bonaparte fall under the above said category.

In modern times there is a general feeling among the people that history has failed to include the role played by the common man in the society. History should not ignore the importance of common man in the society. It should be mentioned in the history. In the Neolithic Age man used to be picking the stone from the earth, but now in the fag end of the 20th century, man is capable of landing on the Moon and Mars, penetrating his eyes through the glass of his scientific advancement and he is reminded of Shakespeare's famous dictum, "what a piece of work man is". It cannot be denied that "man has played a considerable role in the total history of mankind".

Thus, the scope of history, in its restricted sense is nothing but a political history, economic history, social history, and so on. In its broad sense, it is history of the entire world touching all its facets. On the whole history mainly centres round the great events that have had indelible and indestructible mark upon mankind. In short history is concerned with the origin and development of all kinds.

3

Value of History

The question 'what is the use of history?' is often asked by the educated man and the student who is directed to a school of History for his further studies. Every one has to admit at once that in practical way history has no use. As H.S. Commager (The Study of History) points out, "It will not solve problems; it will not guarantee us against the errors of the past; it will not show nations how to avoid wars, or how to win them; it will not provide scientific explanations or keys to prosperity; it will not contribute in any overt way to progress".

It goes without saying that without a knowledge of history, one is denied some of those intellectual and moral experiences which give meaning and richness to life. Without history life would be poorer and meaner.

Of course history is useful in the sense that art and music, poetry and flowers, religion and philosophy are useful.

The uses of history are almost endless. A meaningful social life at present would be impossible without reference to a knowledge of the past. Hence history is necessary.

Moreover History enables us to identify the present with the past. As E.H. Carr in his 'What is History' points out, "History is an unending dialogue between the present and the past". By this one can appreciate the beautiful cities and magnificent buildings. Here the knowledge of the past is very helpful to appreciate the present. So also a study of the medieval trade guilds and the great financial reforms introduced by Ala-ud-din-Khilji in the form of market regulations are immensely useful to understand the present day industrial relations and the price control in modern times respectively. In addition to this the knowledge of the past prepares us to be cautious against the problems that may arise in the future. Hence Sir John Seeley says, "when we learn history, we don't learn the past, but the future."

We learn lessons from history. The organisation of international peace keeping agencies like foe League and the U.N. was born of the lessons drawn from mass human suffering. So Bolingbroke following Dionysius called history 'philosophy teaching by examples'.

In 'The Idea of History' R.G. Collingwood says, 'History has a value; its teachings are useful for human life' simply because the rhythm of its changes is likely to repeat itself, similar antecedents leading to similar consequences; the history of notable events is worth remembering in order to serve as a basis for prognostic judgements, not demonstrable but probable, laying down not what will happen, but what is likely to happen indicating the points of danger in rhythms now going on". In short he says that 'history is for human self-knowledge'.

The new nations of Asia and Africa take many lessons from history for their peace and progress.

History provides moral and ethic values also, Great persons who have rendered remarkable services to humanity are portrayed in history. A study of history gives a vivid account of the lives of great men like Socrates, Mohammed Prophet, Ignatius Loyala, Confucius and Mahatma Gandhi. Their teachings and preachings are highly responsible for shaping and moulding the character of the public. No doubt history gives a mental discipline.

Historical anecdotes and episodes are frequently used by others. Novelists and literates use them as their themes for dramas, novels and other literary works. For example Shakespeare used many historical incidents in his dramas with glorious imaginations. No wonder Winston Churchill said that he had learned all of his English history out of Shakespeare.

In addition to this we know how history comes alive in the novels of Walter Scott.

History includes many sided development of the people including the political, religious, literary, economic, social and cultural aspects of their lives.

Thus everything has its history and every topic can be represented in a historic setting.

History teaches judgement. In his book "Studying History How and Why" Robert V. Daniels says that "it does this by supplying a knowledgeable background and by training in the technique of criticism and conclusions."

Further history helps us to develop a sense of criticism, that is, to ponder over everything and finding out the truth. According to Peyer Geyl that "Criticism is the first duty of independent scholarship" is to be noted here.

It is obvious that history is useful to the rulers, statesmen, diplomats and administrators. As A.L. Rowse points out, "History gives you the right background for most of the affairs which you will have to deal in the administrative service. The great historians Thucydides and Polybius considered history as a guide for conduct, for it furnished examples and warnings to statesmen. For steering the ship of the state in a right path man has to learn the errors and mistakes committed by others in the past. Hence, he must know that failure is the stepping stone of success in his life.

In history we cannot predict the future as in the case of science. Yet it can point out that under certain circumstances certain things are bound to happen. During the time of Hitler Germany suffered seriously at the hands of Russia because he did not understand the implications of Napoleon's campaign to Moscow.

Historical knowledge helps a statesman to introduce beneficial reforms to his people.

Further History helps us to understand and appreciate the realisation of human dignity and democratic rights. In this connection it is very appropriate to know the idea of Hegel, the great philosopher. He believed that, "history is history of the rise and growth of liberty — from the liberty of some to that of all". From history we are able to know that ancient people enjoyed certain rights. But they were deprived of them by the church officials and Divine Right Kings. This finally led to an awakening, among the masses, which in turn started the revolution and recovered their rights.

History provides the utility of education in a grand scale. Moreover it gives pleasures of contemplation. Sir Thomas Munroe, Trevelyan and others give a graphic picture about the utility history. According to Sir Thomas Munroe, "A few pages of history give more insight into the human mind and in a more agreeable manner than all the metaphysical volumes that ever were published".

Thus, the uses of history cannot be minimised or under estimated in modern times.

4

History and Allied Subjects

All intellectual disciplines are interrelated. If we turn the pages of history we can give enough materials for their relationship between one another.

(1) History and Political Science

Political Science is closely related to history. According to Sir John Seeley. "History is past politics and politics is present History". We know that this is but a half-truth, for the stream of history runs right through and politics is but an aspect of history. A knowledge of history is essential for any one in understanding the evolution of political institutions. The great philosophers like Plato, Aristotle and Machiavelli were able to derive their political ideas by mastering the history of political institutions of the great world. They in turn, gave a new outlook to history. In this connection it is better and fitter to cite the idea of Jean Jacques Rousseau. In his monumental work, 'Social Contact' he emphasised the importance of man in the society: "Man is born free and everywhere he is in chains". Thereby, Rousseau kindled the feelings and sentiments of the French people in establishing a classless society.

There is close affinity between history and political science. To Sir John Seeley "History without political science has no fruit and Political Science without history has no root". Acton has said that "the science of politics is the one science that is deposited by the stream of history like grains of gold in the sands of a river." The river itself is history. But politics deals with but a part of it.

In short the two subjects are the two sides of the same coin, "for all politics is not history as all history is not politics".

(2) History and Economics

Economics is intimately connected with history. The two disciplines are inseparable. The economic history of any period is an essential branch of history and its understanding is really important in understanding the history of any period.

Economics deals with things. Moreover it is concerned with the activities of man. History is the narration of events in the chronological order.

A historian is naturally concerned with the principles of economics.

If any one wants to have an idea of the role played by F.D. Roosevelt in American history, it is essential to go through the various economic measures undertaken by him during the period of 'Depression' which is known as the 'New Deal'. From this it is clear that history and economics are interrelated with one another.

Economics deals with production, distribution and consumption of wealth. Dr. N. Subramanian says that "the institutions of slavery, feudalism, imperialism, capitalism and socialism are such an integral part of human history, that unless a historian has sufficient acquaintance with economic theory his analysis of economic factors cannot be satisfactory". Conversely, an economist has to be acquainted with history of economic thought. The various theories which effect the functioning of society belong to history. In modern times, scholars have come out with the economic interpretation of history which make history and economics get closer. Karl Marx believed that all religious, political and judicial developments in history take place due to economic development.

Moreover historical source materials like price structures, interest rates and wage levels mentioned in ancient and medieval documents and inscriptions are immensely useful to the student of past economics.

The difference between history and economics lies in their approach towards the society. History is mainly concerned with the events. But economics attaches importance to things and their value.

(3) History and Statistics

It goes without saying that Modern economic theory depends largely on statistical data. Now a days the historians are no longer using more or less correct terms like majority of the people, popular support etc., instead they have started using the actual percentage of people and so on.

The historians and scholars have got ample official records which contain valuable data like information regarding movement of people, births and deaths, immigration. This is due to the valuable service rendered by statistics. In this connection Lawrence Stone has beautifully remarked in the following manner: "Statistical measurements is the only means of extracting coherent pattern from the chaos of personal behaviour and of discovering what is a typical specimen and what a spout. Failure to apply such controls has led to much wild and implausible generalisations about social phenomena based upon a handful of striking and well documented examples".

(4) History and Literature

G.M. Trevelyan treated history as a branch of literature. But Barnes and Ranke criticised Trevelyan's approach. To them, history was a distinct field of study by itself. According to them history is full of dates, events and evidences. So it cannot become a branch of literature. From the time of the ancient historians Herodotus and Thucydides to Trevelyan we have a number of historians whose literary art has enhanced the beauty of their historical writing. In the hands of Gibbon History attained an unprecedented and unparalleled literary garb.

In history we get an account of the development of literature and in histories of literature we have an account of historiography. Literary men choose historical themes. The best example is Shakespeare. Historians like Macaulay wrote on literary matters in an exemplary way. His matters on Milton and Addisson are very fine literary pieces.

Literature has close affinity with history in respect of historical novels. For instance the great historical novelist Sir Walter Scott's contributions clearly vindicate and indicate those aspects.

There are other historical novelists who have written historical novels in their own languages. Alexander Dumas and Victor Hugo among the French and Tolstoy the Russian who wrote the illustrious 'War and Peace' are the great examples.

Generally the historical novelists are to be very cautious and watchful. Because the historical novel is a combination of fact and fiction. G.M. Trevelyan opines, "Historical fiction is not history but it springs from history and reacts upon it. Historical fiction writers make the past alive. But it is not to make the events alive and therefore it is not history.

(5) History and Sociology

History and sociology are closely linked. Sociology consists of some anthropology, ancient law, study of primitive social customs and habits and of social institutions. But the two disciplines are concerned with the study of man in the society. The two disciplines differ only in their approach. It is topical rather than chronological. E.H. Carr in his 'What is History' observes "Sociology, if it is to become a fruitful field of study must like history concern itself with the relation between the unique and the general: but it must also become dynamic — a study out of society at rest (for no such society exists) but of social change and development. For the rest, I would only say that the more sociological history becomes and the more historical sociology becomes the better for both. Let the frontier between them be kept wide open for two way traffic".

Sociology is a study of group Life. Sociology aims to describe social behavioural patterns, folkways and mores.

According to H.E. Barnes sociology is the basic social science which can hope to give a generalised view of the social process and of social causation. Like the historians, the sociologists adopted the methods like the sampling techniques and questionaires. In short sociology is more concerned with the general laws about the present whereas history with the unique features of the past.

(6) History and Geography

History and Geography are closely linked. This close link is expressed by Immanuel Kant in the following mahnen 'The description according to time is history, that according to space is geography.... History is narrative, geography is descriptive. Geography and history fill up the entire circumference of our perceptions, geography that of space history that of time".

The influence of geography on history is a subject which every treatise on history deals with in its first chapter. One of the undoubted areas of geographical influence on history is the physical formation of a country. Britain, Japan and Greece are instances of countries with broken coastline. This has facilitated their naval strength and empire building activities.

Renaissance Movement came into existence in Italy due to the geographical factor.

R.V. Nadkami in his 'Rise of the Marathas' says that "the nature of the Maratha country facilitated the rise of the Marathas in the beginning of the 17th century".

The Himalayas and the jungles of Assam have confined foreign invasions of India to the north-west. According to K.M. Panikkar the Himalayas contributed very much to shape the life of the country.

In fact all the countries in the world have been greatly helped by the geographical factors. "The Gobi and Mongolian deserts together with the Himalayas provided an isolation for China".

The Geography of Egypt has preserved her ancient civilisation for the archaeologists' spade and the Sahara has cut off sub. Sahara Africa from contact with the rest of the world — till recently Australia was so thoroughly isolated than the Tasman. Kiwi and the Kangaroo were specimens to other parts of the world.

No doubt the geographical discoveries that took place during the 15th and 16th centuries altered the history of mankind.

Climatology also plays a prominent part in national character formation and influences human beings in their endeavours and achievements. Montesquieu, Buckle and Huntington believed in the effect of climate on civilisation. But in modern times this influence of geography on history can be controlled and even conquered became of scientific technological control over nature. In the later half of the 20th century, man can boast of so many of his achievements. He has made his way to lead a comfortable and if possible luxurious life. But he has not yet found an answer to failure of monsoons, periodical hurricanes and earthquakes.

(7) **History and Biology**

History is related to Biology for many reasons. Evolution is the most common principle for both disciplines. R.G. Collingwood thinks that the evolutionary ideas in science were developed under the impact of history.

Newman's Essay on the development of 'Christian doctrine' published in 1845, Darwin's 'Origin of Species' appeared in 1859 and Marx's Das Capital written in 1867 are concerned with evolution. From the above chronology it is clear that even before Darwin, historians knew of the principle of evolution, not necessarily of the species but of institutions and ideas. Bury also has endorsed this view.

The most notable attempt to work out evolutionary ideas in the realm of social science was that of Marxism. Evolution in science reacted on and confirmed and contributed to the idea of progress in history.

According to Will Durant the struggle for existence and the survival of the fittest go on even today.

Another important thing is biological reproduction. Biological reproduction according to the classical warning of Malthus will overtake food creation.

This warning led to man's struggle against nature to attain parity between available food and number of mouths to be fed.

Thus, History and Biology are closely linked.

(8) **History and Philosophy**

Philosophy influences historical writing. Philosophy is nothing but the pursuit of practical wisdom. It has helped a number of historians like R.G. Collingwood, Hegel, Kant and Toynbee.

Philosophy has an extended meaning also. In this way there can be philosophy of history. Two types of questions are possible in relation to history. One is questions asked within history and the other is questions asked about history. When was the first battle of Panipat fought? This is the former type of question. The ready answer of 1526 is a chronicler's answer; it does not require a historian to do it. But the second type of questions are answered by philosophical historians who are historians proper.

In this way history and philosophy are connected with each other.

(9) History and Psychology

History and Psychology are connected with each other. Psychology is essential for the understanding of particular turning point in history. The greatmen theory in history is based on psychology. Abraham Lincoln, Gandhiji and others have been psycho-analytically studied and strange results achieved. Thus, individual psychology is often approached from the psychoanalytical angle.

The puritanism of Hitler or Aurangzeb, the non-violence of Gandhi etc., have been psycho-analytically studied and strange results achieved. This is called psycho-history.

(10) History and Biography

History has got intimate connection with biography. Biography is a form of history whereas the life history of a person is portrayed by the writer. According to Thomas Carlyle. "The Universal history at its bottom was the work of greatmen". For instance the biography of Charles De Gaulle gave a clear picture of France during the years between 1959 to 1969.

Added to this we can also cite another example. The biography of Mahatma Gandhi would give a narrative account of the multifarious problems faced by the Indians and Gandhi's role in getting independence for them from the British.

(11) History and Anthropology

Anthropology and history are closely related to each other. The former deals about the physical and mental constitutions of human beings. Perhaps understanding the affinity that exists between the two disciplines one inclines to say that man is a social animal. Anthropology also helps history in tracing the origin of the vanishing tribes.

5

History as Science and Art

History has been considered an art from time immemorial. But there had been temptations among historians to regard history as a science. The historians of Victorian era first asserted that history was a science.

Thomal Buckle considered history as a science. He had reduced history to a science by bringing it under the dominion of "one glorious principle of universal and undeviating regularity the law of nature".

Auguste Compte too has endorsed this view.

Ranke of Germany who was very keen and particular that history should be accurate and authentic, wanted history to be treated as a science.

In his inaugural lecture on January — 1903 at Cambridge, J.B. Bury described history as "a science, no less and no more". He further said, "so long as history was regarded as an art, the sanctions of truth could not be severe".

The word science is used in the English speaking world in a delimited sense, namely to refer to physical sciences like Physics, Chemistry etc., The word science is used to indicate any enquiry after knowledge and can be equated with knowledge in its totality as can be seen in the words omniscience, nescience and so forth. In short science is a systemised body of knowledge.

According to some scholars history cannot be called a science. An eminent historian G. M. Trevelyan says, "The study of mankind does not resemble the study of the physical properties of atoms, or the life history of animals. If you find about one atom, you have found out about all atoms. But the life history of one man or even of many individual men, will not tell you the life history of other men. "According to him men are too complicated, too spiritual, too various for scientific analysis; and the life history of millions cannot be inferred from the history of one single man". In this connection A.L. Rowse has rightly pointed out that, "Herodotus and Thucydides, Tacitus and Livy, Clarendon, Hume and Gibbon, Macaulay and Carlyle were all artists and among the foremost writers of their time........ there will always remain history as an art".

(1) There are certain qualities which make history a science. It is true that history and science deal with nature. Moreover "man the subject of all historical studies is the greatest work of nature".

(2) History is scientific in the sense that it employs many methods of enquiry such as

(i) observation,

(ii) classification,

(iii) framing hypotheses and

(iv) analysing evidence before interpreting and reconstructing the past.

(3) History is a social science pertaining to social problems. The best example for this is the "Social History of England" by G.M. Trevelyan. It is a science in a sense that it is mainly concerned with the circumstances under which mankind is put. According to Disraeli the late Prime Minister of England, "Man is not the creative of circumstances, but circumstances are the creative of man" is the right view to be mentioned here.

History is entirely different from the physical sciences on the basis of certain other characteristics. Science deals about nature and its phenomena. "History describes the actions, statements and thoughts of human beings. It has nothing to do with the behaviour of 'dead matter' with which science is concerned". In fact historians deal with ideas. On the other hand, the scientist is really objective for he is concerned with objects outside of himself. "The historian does not have the direct experience of the phenomena which he tries to explain. Napoleon's Moscow expedition cannot be reproduced in a laboratory, as the determination of physical properties of water may be".

Moreover history cannot submit its data to scientific experiments.

From above it is clear that history is not a science.

Further a historian collects his information from the library on the traces of events which were already recorded, whereas a scientist works in the laboratory and makes experiments. Experiments in science can be repeated and tested. But in history it is entirely different.

Another important thing is that objectivity is not possible in history. "Perfect objectivity is never achieved". For instance, naturally German historians used to write the history of first world war in their favour and wrote adverse remarks about the English. When an Arab is entrusted with the writing of the Arab-Israeli conflict, he is likely to write something adverse about Israeli. The scientist is not concerned with this kind of problem. Because his study always centres round the nature and his ultimate goal is to find out the real truth, in which he is specialising.

Prediction in history is out of question. It is another important thing in history. Every historical event is unique and different from every other, that is two events are not similar. For example, the Russian Revolution of 1917, is not similar to the French Revolution of 1789. But it is not the case with science. Scientist looks things at universal angle. Hence it is possible for him to arrive at generalisations which ultimately help him to understand the present in a proper way and predict the future. A scientist can forecast occurrence of an earthquake while a historian cannot predict an event.

In this connection Rickman in his "Meaning in History" rightly points out, "History deals with the sequence of events each of them unique, while science is concerned with the routine appearance of things and aims at generalisations and the establishment of regularities governed by laws".

Finally the historian applies the deductive method, that is "in a historical process many developments are analysed and particular conclusions are arrived at. But the scientist makes use of the inductive method in drawing general propositions from particular cases......."

One of the great idealists R.G. Collingwood points out that history is a branch of knowledge obtained by a methodical study. It is a special kind of science which is concerned with the experiences of human beings. He believes that every event has got two sides, internal and external. The historian must make a clear distinction between inside and outside of an event. For instance one cannot fully understand the invasions of Alexander by the outside details of the invasions. The historian has to bear in mind that Alexander's invasion of India is not a mere event but it led to far-reaching reactions.

In addition to this the positivists put forth the view that history should be treated on a par with science. Therefore they started framing laws for it. In short historical thinking is similar to that of the scientific thinking.

Renowned historians like Carlyle, Macaulay, Trevelyan and Churchill attached much importance to the literary qualities of history. Allan Nevin in his "The Gateway to History" points out, "Like Darwin's book a consummate history unites art and science indissolubly". It is very apt to mention here since history can be called both as an art and a science. Thus, History has to be looked from two angles — as a science as well as an art.

6

Lessons of History

A.L. Rowse, Robert V. Daniels and Will and Ariel Durant have given a graphic picture about the lessons of history. In "The Lessons of History" Will and Ariel Durant point out the various lessons of history to the students of history in particular and the other readers in general. According to A.L. Rowse, "The lessons of history are indeed innumerable, and of all kinds, personal as well as social".

One must know some history in order to understand the world one lives in, or to act with any wisdom and perspective. It is true that with the help of the past one may be able to solve a number of problems relating to society. In the words of Sir John Seeley "when we read history, we do not learn the past, but the future".

Will and Ariel Durant point out, "The present is the past rolled up for action and the past is the present unrolled for understanding'. Since history is primarily concerned with the past, one may be able to find whatever answers about the conduct of human affairs. The Greek and Roman history of the ancient period gives a clear picture of the past events. Of course we get pleasure in reading those events. But at the same time we learn lessons from those events of the history of Greece and Rome. To quote Charles Firth, "Not only it is a branch of learning to be studied for its own sake, but a kind of knowledge which is useful to men in daily life". And Sir Walter Raleigh believed that, "the end and scope of all history being to teach us by example of times past such wisdom as may guide our desires and actions". In this connection Francis Bacon has beautifully remarked thus: "Historians make men wise".

The following are some of the lessons that history teaches to mankind:

Here we are using the term 'lessons' for the warnings that history gives to mankind.

(i) History teaches us modesty. During his life time man has to overcome many problems. He is able to control nature; but it limits him. Man can do many wonders on earth. He can irrigate deserts and air-condition the Sahara. He can build a floating city to cross the ocean. "But a tornado can ruin in an hour the city that took a century to build". If rain becomes too rare civilisation disappears under sand in central Asia. If rain falls too furiously, thousands of people become homeless, "and civilisation will be checked with jungle as in central America". Right from ancient times down to present day man is trying to establish a growing mastery over the earth but in vain.

(ii) History teaches lessons with the help of biology also. The first biological lesson of history is that life is competition. We can see the competition not only in trade and commerce but also in life. Animals eat one another without qualm; civilised men consume one another by due process of law.

Another biological lesson of history is that life is selection. Human beings compete with one another for food or power. Not all are able to achieve success, some succeed and some fail. In the struggle for existence only the fittest survive.

Another biological lesson of history is that life must breed.

Will and Ariel Durant point out that people produce great civilisation because of climate and geographical conditions. "If the Negroes of Africa have produced no great civilisation it is probably because climate and geographical conditions frustrated them. It is not the race that makes the civilisation, it is the civilisation that makes the people".

(iii) In the moral side we learn many lessons from history. In other words history teaches moral lessons. Morals are very essential for the society. For better behaviour, order, security and growth of the members of the society they are very essential. Man should not do sins; he should avoid gambling; he should not commit corruption and other evils. Man learns moral lessons from the past.

(iv) Religions have played a prominent role in human history. There is no community without religion. It is a solace to mankind from time immemorial. To the unhappy, the suffering, the bereaved, the old, it has brought supernatural comforts valued by millions of souls as more precious than any natural aid. In short it is a common medicine to cure the ills of the people in every walk of their life.

(v) According to Karl Marx history is economics in many respects such as rivalry among individuals, groups, classes and states for food, fuel, materials and economic power. Economic factor is very important for history. For instance many revolutions broke out in the world due to the economic conditions. Added to this social cause was also responsible for such revolutions. For instance the French Revolution broke out not because of the powerful writings of Voltaire, Montesquieu and Rousseau. It was due to the dominant role played by the middle class which needed legislative freedom and political power. Further in such revolutions the poor proved stronger than the rich. Particularly in the Russian Revolution of 1917 the Bolsheviks captured power. The Western Asia was conquered by the Mongols. From above we know military victory gave political ascendancy which bought economic control.

Karl Marx has given his beautiful ideas regarding the economic interpretation of history. History also points out there will always be the struggle between the 'haves' and the have-nots'. He also points out the class-struggle in history. The rich and the poor are two different poles. There is no possibility of the two getting closer.

(vi) We learn many lessons from the political organisations like 'Monarchy, tyranny, Aristocracy, Oligarchy, Dictatorship and Democracy'. Power corrupts society *i.e.*, people absolutely. Man was bound to be a slave for such power. Finally such power led to his downfall. Even today it is happening in the politics of the world.

(vii) From history we learn that neither success nor failure is everlasting. It is better and fitter to cite the case of Napoleon Bonaparte here. He met success after success in many places in Europe in the very beginning of his career; in the same continent he met great failure in 1815 (The Battle of Waterloo) at the end of his career. Thus his hopes were shattered to pieces. He was imprisoned in St. Helena till his death in 1821. This teaches a lesson to the future heroes of history.

(viii) From history we learn that the victors have always suppressed the vanquished. The best example for this is the Treaty of Versailles of 1919. Accordingly Germany was crippled and crushed by the victors. Another example is the condition of Japan after the Second World War. The Japanese cities were completely destroyed (Hiroshima and Nagasaki) by atom bombs. It was humiliated and brought under American control. But within a short span of years it equipped itself in very many fields. Today it is a leading power and a force to reckon with in the world arena.

(ix) History teaches some lessons to the civilised world. According to Will and Ariel Durant "History is a subject that rids you of illusion, and in which you grow up and become adult".

(x) From history we learn lessons from extreme nationalism and imperialism.

To put it in a nutshell history offers many lessons to the people now and then from past experiences.

7

Abuses of History

History is more often misused and abused rather than being properly used. It is a general opinion prevalent in the society. There are many events in history; so also there are many incidents in history; but in the process of recording and reconstructing they are misused. This may be due to the following reasons:

(1) The 20th century historian writes about events over which he had no direct contact or connection. For example when he is writing on the 1857 uprising in the history of Modern India he entirely depends upon original sources and contemporary witnesses for their accurate observation and reliable information. Of course the persons who provide the information are liable to human errors and prejudices. In this attempt we can also see fabricated versions. People were made to believe that the world would come to an end in the year 1000 A. D. Later on it was proved in the 19th century by a Benedictine monk that this episode had never happened.

(2) For the abuse of history superstition has contributed very much. Some writers in the past were highly responsible in giving a very high place to divine forces for all happenings. The best examples are the Mahabharata and the Ramayana. In addition to this the role of the divine forces has been very much exaggerated by the writers like St. Paul, Cardinal Newman and St. Augustine. Gradually this conception gained momentum in history. Finally this conception paved the way for the philosophy of history.

Great political thinkers like Hegel and Karl Marx came forward with the truth. But this does not hold good.

(3) Generally history is misused by the political parties to serve their needs and interests. "During the Reformation movement the Protestants and the Catholics used history to show the working of God's Providence in accordance with their own predilections....." In the same manner history was used as a tool by the competing

interests in the past and in the present it is used as a tool in the same way by the competing interests.

(4) The contribution of new movements and turning points in history to the misuse of history cannot be minimised or under estimated. For example the outbreak of French Revolution and the Russian Revolution brought significant changes. Historians described the struggle between the haves and have-nots in writing those Revolutions. But there is no element of truth behind their writings. They properly did so in order to advance their causes.

(5) Political and economic trends also make the writers to distort historical facts. In the 18th and 19th centuries nationalism arose in many countries of the world. It greatly helped in writing the histories of individual countries. In such histories we find national glorification and a corresponding denigration of other people.

(6) Individual writers misuse history to serve their needs and interests. Historical writers distort history because of bias, opportunism and fear. In England some historians like Macaulay wrote their histories from the Whig point of view; some other historians wrote from the Tory point of view. It should be avoided for an impartial history of that country.

The court historians like Abul Fazl patronised by the Mughal rulers had written historical works in colourful languages, high style, glorifying whatever they did.

In short history is not totally free from the evils of misuse and abuse. Hence the saying which runs thus: "Historians are dangerous. They are capable of upsetting everything. They must be directed".

8

Philosophy of History

In the 18th century Voltaire the great French Philosopher used this term Philosophy of History with reference to critical history. He meant by it according to Collingwood, 'no more than critical or scientific history; a type of historical thinking in which the historian made up his mind for himself instead of repeating whatever stories he found in old books'. He has expressed this view in his 'Idea of History'. Hegel used the term to signify the universality of history. Positivists used the term to indicate the discovery of general laws governing the course of events. In his book "What is History" E.H. Carr says that "History is a continuous process of interactions between the historian and his facts, an unending dialogue between the present and the past".

History-Nature: In order to define the Philosophy of history, we must be very clear about what history is and what philosophy has got to say about history. It is true that "historical thinking is a special kind of thinking concerned with the past". When philosophy deals with history, it has to take into consideration the mind of the historian and the nature of the facts. Philosophy serves as a guiding factor for the thinkers in many respects.

The philosophy of a people depends upon the history of the people. Now and then there has been sufficient interaction between the history of a people and a philosophy of a people. Droysen says that, "history is the 'know Thyself of humanity — the self-consciousness of mankind". From the study of Aryan settlements and the Dravidian culture we get their profound philosophical reflections and finer values respectively. At times of stresses and strains men like Buddha and Mahavira restored dignity. Their message of hope and awakening restored a faith in the values of life to change the course of events not only in India but in many parts of the then civilised world.

In addition the successive waves of migration and conquests brought to this land not only varied pattern of living but diverse value of thinking as well.

Philosophy-Nature: Philosophy is considered a way of life. It is a guideline for the present and the future. From the earliest times philosophy dealt with reflections on theology and on the relations between God and man. The people very easily began to understand the values of Buddha and Jesus Christ in this connection. They satisfied themselves with veracity of religious beliefs.

Philosophy of History: G.M. Trevelyan said that there is no philosophy of history. 'Philosophy must be brought to history, it cannot be extracted from it'.

There are two views with regard to the philosophy of history. "In the broad spectrum of recent historiography, Voltaire and Hegel wanted philosophy of history to stand for certain ideas and functions to which history alone could be relevant; but the positivists were trying to make history not a philosophy but an empirical science like meteorology". Thus to the latter, Philosophy of history meant the discovery of uniform laws and to the former independent and critical thinking. R.G. Colling wood disagrees with both and said that "all history is the history of thought" and that "history is the re-enactment in the historians mind of the thought whose history he is studying."

There are two views of history, one teleological and the other eschatological. These two views would destroy the secular nature of history .

The ecological interpretation of history partakes of the character of myth. "The interpretation is outside history altogether. Grant all that theology claims, that Rome fell and England arose, that America was discovered or was so long undiscovered because God wills it".

The materialistic interpretation of history is that human beings whatever their beginning have emerged by very slow degrees from the condition of animals and all their knowledge has been gathered by experience. This experience has formed the human character which determined the course of human history.

The transcendent view of history is that history has a meaning beyond appearances. Croce said 'the search for the transcendental end is the philosophy of history'. The question of generalisation in history is cardinal. It is associated with the question of the lessons of history.

There is a view that history is the unfolding story of human freedom. This view prevailed in the 19th century. Lord Acton was an illustrious exponent of this view.

Another concept related to this theory is the 'Greatman Theory'. It is the mechanic who operates the wheel of history. Carlyle was the greatest exponent of this view. To him the hero was the demi god. Will Durant has advocated a qualified hero theory. Accordingly human progress is due to the work of great men like generals, statesmen, saints or intellectuals. Contrary to this we have the concept of superman.

It goes without saying that the philosophy of history is a search for a meaning in history. I. Berlin and M. Powicke support this view. According to C.A. Beard the philosophy of history is 'the investigation of the rational principles which it is assumed are disclosed in the historical process due to the cooperation and interaction of human minds under terrestrial conditions.'

During the 19th Century it led to the formation of social theories by Saint Simon, Compte, Marx, Vico, Herder and Montesquieu.

Speculative and Critical History: The term philosophy of history has meant two things — speculative and critical. Speculative historians probe into the past in order to determine the driving force of events. This is done with the belief that there must have been some connected link which gradually unfolds the drama of human life. Critical historians seek to understand the conflicting nature of events and veracity and objectivity in the study of history. Men like Hegel and Marx, Spengler and Toynbee, Collingwood and Carr postulate different propositions for the historical events and though no last word can be said on the subject, the differing view points themselves fascinate the studies and towards reaching a better perspective of history.

The views expressed by giant figures on the philosophy of history are not idle speculations on history. Their opinions gradually shape the course of mankind itself. Ideas are powerful weapons used by great statesman to change the destiny of nations. Ideologies, in course of time, become effective instruments in the annals of international relations.

The concept of the philosophy of history began roughly speaking with the Romanticists though they did not create the concept. Herder's 'Ideas for the philosophy of the history of humanity', Kant's 'Idea of universal History', Schlegel's 'Philosophy of History" and Friedrich Krause's 'General Philosophy of History' describe vividly the concept of the philosophy of history.

According to Theodore Jouffroy changes in human ideas underlie and determine all other phases of human development.

In England Edmund Burke, Herbert Spencer, H.T. Buckle, Bagehot and Leslie Stephen have made some contribution of peripheral nature to this subject.

The most eminent application of Hegelian dialectic to create the materialistic interpretation of history was that of Marx who said in effect that economic factors ultimately determine human and social development.

During the early periods 'Providence' the benign word was used to explain the historical facts. All that happened in the past was attributed to divine will. Jewish historians followed this idea. Hegel's unfolding of Reason attracted the attention of the scholars. He enthroned Reason as the grand Arbiter and opined that the triumph of Reason as the lesson of history. In short the philosophies of history have been concerned with discovery of past, interpretation of historical phenomena, speculation about the ultimate nature of history and so forth.

9

Branches of History

History includes many sided development of the people including the political, economic, religious, scientific, social and cultural aspects, of their lives. So "history is the story of human society, or the stories of human societies. Upon that ground work all the variety and detail of history arise". Hence G.M. Trevelyan opines that, "History is not a subject at all but a house in which all subjects dwell".

In 'The Study of History' H.S. Commager rightly points out, "there are as many kinds of history as there are historians and each historian writes his own kind of history". From this it is very clear that there are many kinds of history. They are:

(i) Political History
(ii) Constitutional History
(iii) Legal History
(iv) Diplomatic History
(v) Military History
(vi) Economic History
(vii) Social History
(viii) Universal History
(ix) Intellectual History.

Let us analyse one by one the above varieties of history.

(i) *Political History:* Traditionally political history has been the favourite branch of history. A.L. Rowse points out that "Politics consists of the public behaviour of man in the masses; it is the society's sphere of action. It is of central importance in the life of a society. And similarly political history must always be the backbone of history". The great historians like Thucydides, Gibbon and Macaulay have attached great importance to political history.

A good part Of human life has been in the past and even now is dominated by the activities of politicians whether they be Monarchs or

Presidents or Prime Ministers, members of samitis or sabhas, folkmoots or parliaments. Political history as the record of public events, the lives of the leading men who took part in them, attracts any individual in the society. It is true that almost all history is now studied in a political framework.

In ancient period, in the society the people used to elect one among them as their chief or leader. Later on the leaders or 'Supreme among equals misused their power, calling themselves as representatives of God on earth. They created anarchy and conclusion in the society'.

In modern period we have senates and parliaments. Their function is to act as the common man's representative to look after the welfare of the former. Then we have the occasional genius, the greatman, the hero who by virtue of his 'charisma' leads others in the society.

During the ancient and medieval times, politics got the lion's share of the historian's attention because most of the source material for those periods can be derived from court records, accounts of court chroniclers or born flatterers like Abul Fazl, royal orders and royal edicts. Of course there are other source materials like dealing with other matters like ecclesiastical chronicles dealing with church histories and so forth. But prominent persons' accounts become prominent and therefore easily accessible to a historian. Humble persons' histories are not given importance by historians. It is due to the lack of source materials. But "Political history is the mainstream of all history" and it is a necessary back drop for any other kind of history as stated by Dr. N. Subramanian.

In the third quarter of the twentieth century, historians no longer attach importance to the political aspect of History for an individual in the society can shape his own destiny and a ruler is no longer considered as 'master' instead 'the first servant' of the state.

For national pride and patriotism political history is very essential and hence it is very popular. Macaulay's 'History of England', Michelet's 'History of France', John Muller's 'History of the Swiss Confederation', Henry Adam's 'History of the United States during the administration of Jefferson and Madison' and Roy Chaudhuri's 'Political History of Ancient India' are considered as best examples on political history.

There are some drawbacks in approaching history through politics. According to H.S. Commager, "The political approach to history is fraught with danger". It paves the way for narrow approach to history. It inculcates parochial view of history. It finally tempts both historian and student to indulge in patriotism. Moreover it exaggerates the role of politics and diplomacy of the expense of other elements in history. Finally it ignores culture, religion, social and economic institutions. It cannot be denied that political history is considered as the mainstream of all history in the world.

(ii) *Constitutional History*: Next to political history constitutional history is very important. It helps the people to understand the society in its proper perspective. In "The Uses of History" A.L. Rowse points out "constitutional history gives the story of the society's institutions, the political and administrative frame work that helps the society together and enables it to work". Constitution here means the political constitution of the ruler and conventions which govern the activities of the government, the rights and duties of the citizens, law and the mode of justice, the executive functions of the state, the economic and financial implications of the government, and the nature of the bureaucracy that will govern the people and so forth.

Besides there are written documents. Some countries have written constitutions and others have unwritten constitutions. We have written constitution in our country. In England there is no written constitution, but there are numerous statutes which express the governmental philosophy of the people. In short constitutional history is mainly concerned with the origin and growth of political institutions like the parliament, the bureaucracy and so on.

Prof. Dicey's 'Law of the Constitution' is an illustrious example for the historical narrative of the origin and growth of the principles of constitutionalism.

From biographies of leading men also we get material for constitutional history.

A.L. Rowse compares the constitutional history with the history of a species or a family in natural science. In the 19th Century many great constitutional historians like Hallam, Comewall Lewis, Stubbs and Maitland were very much in touch with the life and the kind of affairs they were writing about. For instance, "Comewall Lewis was a cabinet Minister of many offices, Stubbs a bishop" . Their way of writing gives a clear picture of public affairs in their life. But the constitutional histories written after them were by people out of touch with affairs, the denizens of libraries rather than of cabinets. Hallam's constitutional history is filled with the sense of the living issues of the day. Maidand was an ideal specialist researcher. It was full of life and brilliance. His new trials happened to be detective stories to the historians. Some historians make a distinction between constitutional and administrative history.

(iii) *Legal History*: Generally speaking Rule of Law is the way of life in all civilised societies. In short all are equal before law. Law plays a prominent and predominant role in the lives of men. If there is no law and order there is bound to erupt chaos and confusion. There will be anarchy and lawlessness. People may not have a comfortable living. The following works have come out on the subject:

(a) Commentaries on the Laws of England by Blackstone (1790).

(b) History of English Law by Holdsworth (in fourteen volumes).

(c) Contributions of Pollard and Maitland.

(d) Laws of Manu (History of the Codification of Laws).

(e) Justinian's Code.

(f) Napoleonic Code.

(g) Code of Hammurabi.

(h) History of the Dharmasastras by P.V. Khanna.

The above contributions are very useful and helpful to know the legal history.

(iv) *Diplomatic History*: Diplomatic history is a specialised branch of political history. It is one of the branches of political history. This emerges as a special discipline in the field of international relations. Diplomacy is conducted by the ambassadors. They are the links between nations and they are the custodians and practitioners of diplomacy. How they have been doing it constitutes diplomatic history.

In modern times foreign affairs play even a dominant role in the affairs of many nations. The foreign policy of a country towards another country create world situations like the cold war, regional groupings of power which ultimately ends up in a world organisation like the United Nations.

In the present century diplomatic history has attained full fledged form. Henry Barr's 'Evolution of Humanity' and Hammertion's 'A universal history of the world' are considered good works on the subject. Thus diplomatic history has its own field of specialisation.

(v) *Military History*: This is no doubt a part of political history. Waging of war has been a political activity. Military history is primarily concerned with the causes of war, strategy and tactics in war, war weapons, decisive battles and other matters associated with warfare. From ancient times historical writings like, 'The History of the Peloponnesian War' by Thucydides, 'The Great Rebellion' by Clarendon have dealt with military themes. In the 20th century, a number of works have been made towards this aspect of history. V.D. Savarkar's "The First War of Indian Independence', A J.P. Taylor's 'Origin of the Second World War' Winston Churchill's 'History of the Second World War' and 'The America Civil War" and 'The Indian Mutiny' are worth remembering in this field of study.

(vi) *Economic History*: Economic history is considered as another favourite branch of history. H.S. Commager in his monu-mental work "The Study of History" says that "A rough and ready working distinction can be made by saying that economic history tells you how a society produces a livelihood".

Economic history is connected with ways and means by which a society gains its subsistence, its land system, and method of agriculture; its industries, trade, business, its financial institutions, communications, conditions of labour and its mode of organisation and so on.

William Ashley defines economic history in the following manner:

"Economic history, the history of man's Economic activity is the history of the utilisation by man of his environment, to obtain therefrom subsistence and the satisfaction of those material wants which are bound up with subsistence".

In history economic factors play a prominent role in very many aspects. In other words economic history deals with economic factors in history. Man needs comfortable and convenient life in the society. To achieve this he has to work hard and whatever he does is equal to his economic activity. Besides he wants to get glory and form in his life. Yet he gives primary importance to economics. The social unequality that led to the struggle between the wealthy and poor created a cloudy atmosphere in France during the French Revolution can be cited as the best example here. Finally this struggle led to the fall of the Bastille on 14th July 1789 in France. The then ruler Louis XVI failed to provide bread for the people when they shouted for bread. As a result of this they witnessed the outbreak of the French Revolution in 1789. Apart from this many good and beneficent rulers also experienced economic problems in their reign. For instance the reign of Shah Jahan which is generally called the golden age of the Mughal rule did have economic problems. There was severe and serious famine in Gujarat during his reign which undermined the power of the ruler. Hence Edwardes and Garratt says it, "The reign of Shah Jahan sounded the death knell of the Empire and of the economic system". From above we can get a clear idea as to how economic factors affect the society at its roots.

Today we see many developed countries and under developed countries in the world. These are due to their economic growth and development. The underdeveloped countries get, economic aid and assistance from the United Nations.

Much attention has not been given for economic history. In other words for long, economic history has been neglected by scholars and writers. Charles Darwin and Karl Marx came to the forefront to explain the importance of economic factors in the national and international politics. Karl Marx advocated the 'Materialistic interpretation of history'. He further said that the historical process is determined by the economic background. In short the history of all societies is the history of class struggle according to Karl Marx.

The following books are noteworthy on this subject:

(a) 'The Economic Organisation of England' by William Ashley.

(b) 'The Growth of English Industry and Commerce' by William Cunningham.

(c) 'Life and Labour of the people in London' by Charless Booth.

Thus, Economic history is considered as the favourite branch of history.

(vii) *Social History*: Social history depicts the history of human society. It deals with the social aspect of the historical problems. As N. Subramanian rightly points out, "Social history must include all the activities of that society which cannot include constitutional, diplomatic or political histories". In his "Social History of England" G.M. Trevelyan has given a definition of social history *i.e.*, "it is the history with the politics left out".

G.M. Trevelyan says that social history describes the daily life of the inhabitants of the land in past ages. He further adds that "without social history, economic history is barren and political history is unintelligible". In his monumental work 'The Social History of England' (the five centuries) he has given a graphic picture of various institutions and the general condition of the people of England.

Social history is concerned with the origin and development of institutions. It functions in two ways. Firstly social history used its source materials in tracing the origin of institutions and records the stages of their development. Secondly, from a thorough study of those institutions as they function now, it makes a retrospective study.

Now-a-days importance has been given to social history. Society in the past is connected to the society in the present. More things have been taken from the past to test the present in very many fields. If we go through the 'Social History of England' by Trevelyan we will get a fairly viable and vivid picture of the evolving English society.

Macaulay in the third chapter of his 'History of England' almost pioneered a sort of social history of England of those times, and John Richard Green in his 'Short History of the English People' indicated the development of English civilisation. Besides A.L. Rowse's 'The Elizabethan Age', E. Hughes's 'North Country life in the Eighteenth Century' and 'International Social History' edited by J.H. Plumb are the most interesting works in this field of study.

'Hindu Polity' by K.P. Jayaswal, 'South Indian polity' by T.V. Mahalingam and 'Sangam Polity' by N. Subramanian are very worthy contributions of our country in the line of social history.

There are certain problems in social history. They are: its continuity, the slowness and subtlety of its changes. According to G.M. Trevelyan, "social change moves like an underground river, Obeying its own laws or those of economic changes rather than following the direction of political happenings that move on the surface of life. Politics are the outcome rather than the course of social changes. A new King, a new Prime Minister, a new Parliament often makes a new epoch in politics but seldom in the life of a people. How then is the tale to be told."

In social history we find in every period several different kinds of social and economic organisation in different places. However, it gives a through knowledge of those different periods to us. Thus, social history occupies a prominent place in modern times.

(viii) *Universal History*: Universal history is otherwise called total history. It is a recent development in historical writing. This will be a sort of world History. The sheer magnitude of the effort is bound to discourage even the hardiest among working historians. In the words of G.R. Elton, "All good history writing is universal history in the sense that it remembers the universal while dealing with a part of it." H.G. Wells tried something like this in his "Outline of History" and he failed. The sheer impossibility of doing any justice to such a subject must concern historians away from this job. In this contest we should remember the Buckle's famous book 'History of Civilisation in England.' Will Durant did succeed in his venture by producing his monumental work, 'Story of Civilisation.' The UNESCO recently started an ambitious scheme of writing the cultural history of mankind. It is called history of mankind, cultural and scientific development. Many contributors are rendering remarkable service to this great project. But this project has its adverse critics also. Thus, universal history is very attractive and informative.

(ix) *Intellectual History* : According to H.E. Barnes Intellectual history seeks to review the transformations of ideas, beliefs and opinions held by the intellectual classes from primitive times to our own (A history of historical writing by H.E. Barnes). It is better and fitter to cite a few works produced on this kind of history. 'An Intellectual and Cultural History of the Western World' (3 volumes) written by H.E. Barnes and others is an illustrious one, some would prefer to call this history, the history of ideas. There are also works on particular aspect of human thought. Works on historiography and the history of the development of historical thought, history of political thought, history of economic thought, history of mathematics and the history of science and technology belong to this category.

Here Das Gupta's 'History of Indian Philosophy' and R.G. Collingwood's 'Idea of History' are noteworthy examples for History of the Ideas. From this we know all aspects of human life.

Schillar said "the genuine history of mankind is its history of ideas" is to be remembered here. He further adds that "It is ideas that distinguish men from all other beings. Ideas endanger social institutions, political changes, technological methods of production, and all that is called economic condition".

R.G. Collingwood was of the opinion that "History is the expression of human ideas".

Carl G. Gustavson said "ideas may be described as the ultimate given of history, for organised social movements cannot appear and institutions cannot function without ideas. They are the cords which bind the minds of men together sufficiently for joint action to occur".

10

Nature of Causation — Does History Repeat Itself?

Every historian is very anxious to know the causes of things. Historians are not content merely with recording what happened, they want to explain why it happened. As H.S. Commager points out, "of all problems of history, causation is the most urgent, the most fascinating and the most baffling".

The following questions have been raised by many philosophers and historians for which they have laboured hard to answer such questions about the cause of History:

(1) Why did the American colonies break away from Great Britain?

(2) What were the causes that led to the success of the thirteen colonies in their revolution?

(3) Why did the southern states wish to break away from the American Union?

(4) Why was their revolution unsuccessful?

(5) Why do only English speaking peoples have two party system while all others have a one or multi-party system?

(6) What were the causes for the two world wars? Generally the enquiry has been open and independent.

Many historians inquired into the causes of things. The Greek and Roman historians rarely did this. They thought that it was all in the hands of gods or of fate. Even the great historian Thucydides does not seek to deeper causes of the Peloponnesian war or the defeat of Athens. According to E.H. Carr "even Thucydides has been accused of having no clear conceptions of causation".

St. Augustine in his 'City of God' used history for illustrating the plan and purpose of God. According to him "history was nothing but the story of the great struggle between the City of God and the City of Satan in which that God would ultimately win."

It was believed that all things happened due to will of God. In the same manner French historian too prepared his 'Discourse on Universal History'.

Historians and philosophers of history began to find out the causes of historical events. "Sometimes the causes and the laws were thought of in mechanical, sometimes in biological terms, sometimes as metaphysical, sometimes as economic, sometimes as psychological".

Now it is better to see how the historians are making use of the causes. Firstly the historian will commonly assign several causes to the same event. For the out break of French Revolution in 1789 and the Russian Revolution in 1917 historians give many causes. Moreover we see that historians deal with multiple causes. Secondly the historian after compiling the causes over an event reduces it to order. Edward Gibbon attributed the decline and fall of the Roman Empire to the triumph of barbarism and religion. The English Whig historian of the 19th Century attributed the role of the British power and prosperity to the development of political institutions embodying the principles of constitutional liberty. Gibbon and the 19th century historians have ignored the economic causes to which modern historians give utmost importance. As E.H. Carr rightly opines, "Every historical argument revolves round the question of the priority of causes".

'Determination in History' and 'Chance in History' are the two theories closely attached to the causes of events in history. The other source of attack is the famous cause of 'Cleopatra's nose'. The results of the battle of Actium were due to Antony's infatuation wife Cleopatra is attributed by many historians. At the same time it is not quite correct to point out feat Antony's defeat and the fall of the Roman Empire were due to Cleopatra's beauty. From this it is clear feat sequences of cause and effect are clashing wife one another. Moreover the first historian to insist on the role of chance in history was Polybius. After feat Gibbon and Bury followed the same.

It is the duty of the historians to select and marshall facts. Not all facts are historical facts. A similar process can be applied in the historian's approach to causes. This will lead to same clue to the problem of the accidental in history. The shape of Cleopatra's nose and the premature death of Lenin at the age of 54 were accidents which modified the course of History. To put it in a nutshell everything feat happens in history has a cause. "A cause is a convenient figure of speech for any one of a number of factors which helps to explain why a historical event happened".

Does History Repeat Itself ?

No doubt in science experiments can be repeated. But past experience in history cannot be repeated. These are very simple propositions. We come across often the dictum "history repeats itself". The real reason is that every historical event is unique. Historical situations involve human beings, one man's habits, thinking and outlook may be entirely different from the other. As G.M. Trevelyan aptly says, 'If you find out about one atom, you have found out about all atoms and what is true of the habits of one robin is roughly true of the habits of all robins. But the life story of one man, or even of many individual men will not tell you life history of other men'.

A superficial observer with little historical sense will say that the Russian Revolution was the repetition of the French Revolution or that the second world war was that of the first. There can be only occurrence of similar situations and not identical situations. We find in history that a few situations have the very similar circumstances. For instance even in the history of India when we notice that after the death of Louis XIV, weak and inefficient rulers occupied the throne. It is the very same case in the history of India when we notice that after the exit of Aurangzeb, Bahadur Shah I and Alam Shah. But even then there is no warrant for the statement that history repeats itself. Therefore it may be said that history not only does not repeat itself but even cannot repeat itself.

Of course some lessons are drawn from history. The utility of drawing such lessons from history will not repeat itself. If the lesson is a warning it can be used to insulate the similar features in future situations. N. Subramanian gives a beautiful illustration which runs thus: An overwhelmingly illiterate and politically uneducated adult population if clothed with electoral franchise will lead to despotism? This is a warning which Walter Bagehot gave.

Britain drew a lesson from the facts of earlier empires and before she could be compelled to forcibly part with it, gracefully gave it up. E.H. Carr says. "One reason why history rarely repeats itself among historically conscious people is that the Dramatist personae are aware at the second performance of the Denouement of the first and their action is affected by that knowledge."

11

Role of Individuals and Ideas

Individuals are highly responsible for shaping the course of history. All historical events involve a large part of human element. The following two theories are very important in this respect.

(1) The heroes of histories are considered as the agents of 'Providence'. The foremost mover in this case is the divine power or natural force. This divine power picks out certain individuals and employs them for the attainment of desired goals. One incumbent after another take the task of fulfilling the goals. To make the view clear Sidney Hook cites an example. According to him, as far as the divine influence on the development of Europe is concerned, Columbus was the first to discover America. In case his ships would not have reached the shores of America, the new world would have been discovered any how.

(2) The 'Greatmen Theory' is the second concept in this respect. From time to time many great men appear in the world and cause great changes. They are the reformers, conquerers, saints and thinkers. They are the most prominent and predominant men in the history. They are history making or event-making people. They are highly responsible for making major upheavals in society.

A distinction should be made between the 'event-making man and the 'eventful' man. Usually the event-making man is a genius. He has unusual talents and gifts. Great leaders belong to the category. On the other hand the eventful man is different. Only situation makes him a hero. For example, the little Dutch boy who kept his finger in the hole of the dikes and saved the town, may the compared to the role of an eventful man. There have been several monarchs in history who have been more or less the tools of historical process. We can cite the King of England, Henry VIII as an example for this. He allowed himself to be an agent of the historical process which brought about the break of the English Church with the Catholic Church of Rome.

It is believed that individual leadership may arise out of several circumstances. They are:

(1) leadership and authority may be inherited.

(2) leaders may emerge by sheer force of their ideas. Example Gandhiji.

(3) leaders may emerge through the institutions of community.

Besides the course of history may take a turn on account of action or inaction. Due to positive action many decisive changes take place in the historical process. We can cite many examples for this positive action. One such was the Nehru's Policy of industrialisation. The result was the formulation and implementation of a series of Five Year Plans. For inaction we can cite the example of Louis XVI of France. He negatively contributed to the Revolution by his apathy and inaction. Due to the weakness of Nicholas II the Bolshevik Revolution of Russia broke out in 1917.

Thus the individuals play a prominent role in the historical process.

The Role of Ideas: In the historical process ideas play a significant role in every respect. Many philosophers and thinkers gave good ideas from time to time.

There are two categories of ideas. They are theoretical and practical.

Theoretical ideas are philosophical in content and character. They are mostly in the form of hypotheses which cannot be readily verified. They are beyond the range of rational analysis, for example Fate, Karma etc. They have to be taken or rejected depending upon individual conviction. We cannot experiment with those ideas. In short they lie beyond the scope of empirical analysis.

Practical ideas can be verified and authenticated. They can be accepted or rejected on the basis of known proofs. They have great importance and value in the day-to-day life of men. Illustrations of the practical ideas that influence men, are the ideas of monarchy, capitalism, socialism and democracy etc.

The above ideas first emerge in the minds of dreamers and thinkers. Gradually they gain momentum or get rejected. Generally a lasting idea or concept thrives more in the face of challenge. An idea that is not repeatedly challenged often decays and disappears. If an idea is constantly attacked, it definitely develops lasting qualities by creating firm convictions in the minds of the people. For example, all great ideas from Christianity to communism have flourished only in the face of opposition and challenge.

It goes without saying that every social, political and economic institution has at the back of it a successful idea.

The ideas of the thinkers, philosophers and reformers are often in conflict with the existing traditions, values and conventions. They are unpopular since they are in the minority. So they face prosecution at the hands of vested interests. Long after their time, the course of history indicates their ideas. During short span of his life time Marx failed to reap the fruit of his labour. But later on practical man like Lenin made Marxism a living reality. Thus ideas play a prominent role in historical process.

12

The Concept of Progress

The word 'Progress' is derived from the two Latin words 'Pro' and 'Gradi' (meaning forward and walk respectively). The word 'Progress' therefore means walk forward and signifies movement at required pace on a desired and desirable direction. In history the concept of progress has been interpreted differently at different times. In ancient India, the Hindus believed in a cyclical movement going from one era to the next to complete the cycle of four eras and then returning to the starting point. Christian theology believes in linear progress. God appears on the scene at the end of the world and meets out reward or punishment depending upon the individual's bad or good acts. Ancient Greeks also took the same view. But the theory of continuous human development leading to perfection as a result of man's own efforts is a modern concept.

The concept of progress is of recent origin. The Christians postulated a goal forwards which the historical process is moving. It was a teleological view of history, the meaning and purpose of which was beyond the secular process of history. Kingdoms rise and fall in order that the purpose of God regarding man might be realised. In the 'City of God', St. Augustin elaborates this idea in a beautiful manner. It made the fall of Adam the turning point of human history.

The idea of progress has been accepted by all in all the ages. Moreover the era of Enlightenment in France witnessed the future development of the idea of progress. The Enlightenment thinkers and the Encyclopaedists had great faith in the progress and in the perfectibility of man.

During the period of Renaissance classical view was restored in which secularism had a firm footing.

During the British period the cult of progress reached its apex. A protagonist of the cult, Lord Acton called history 'a progressive science'.

According to C. A. Beard the idea of progress exercised a great influence in modern times.

Bury made classic contribution to the idea of progress in his famous book "The Idea of Progress". He describes progress as the animating and controlling idea of western civilisation.

In his great work "What is History" E.H. Carr sums up the main elements of the concept of progress. He says that history is progress through the transmission of acquired skills from one generation to another. Here "acquisition" is given more importance than "inheritance". It comes through evolution. The evolutionary process is very slow. But that is not the case with the other. In addition to this progress does not have a definite beginning nor a definite end. It is a continuous process. At the same time we cannot precisely point the starting point of progress. It is believed that Nile valley in the 4th Millennium B.C. was the cradle of civilisation. Even this belief is no longer popular. But the beginning go further deep into the twilight of history. Thus for the historian 'progress is a never-ending process'. Apart from this progress never takes place in a straight unbroken line, without reverses or deviations.

Condorcet, Compte, Vico and Mill have given their ideas about progress.

Bury describes the idea of progress as a theory which evolves a synthesis of the past and a prophecy of the future. It is better to be remembered here, a civilisation grows and declines, then takes a new birth and marches forward perhaps at a different time and place.

It cannot be denied that the ancient people equated progress with divine benevolence. Their goal was divine Heaven. In the 18th century the scholars conceived progress in terms of freedom and democracy. In the 20th century the concept of progress has come to be identified with conquest of nature. By this their aim is to improve the standard of living.

According to E.H. Carr progress in one direction is offset by regression in another. It is not true. Man has to face many challenges amidst many calamities and conflicts. In spite of all these trials and tribulations he gets success due to his faith in progress.

13

Ancient Historiography

(A) GREECE

(i) Herodotus : The earliest tradition of historiography belongs to the Greeks. Greek history proper begins in the 6th century B.C. Herodotus was the first Greek historian to recognise the value of the important international episodes and he developed a system by which he could omit the irrelevant and spotlight the major events. He was the author of the first universal history.

Herodotus was born in an aristocratic family of Halicarnassus in South West Asia Minor, sometimes between 490 and 480 B.C. He spent most of his time in travel. He visited almost all Greek cities. Wherever he went he collected materials for his great work on the Persian invasion of Greece.

Later on Herodotus migrated to Athens. During the time of Pericles the city rose in power and prestige. He lived to see the beginning of the death struggle between Athens and her rivals in the Pelaponnesian War. He died at the age of sixty.

In the 'History of the Persian Wars', Herodotus endeavoured "to preserve from decay and remembrance of what men have done and to prevent the great and wonderful actions of the Greeks and the barbarians from loosing their due need of glory". He wrote this book on the basis of "his eyes, his judgement and his talent for enquiry". He succeeded in writing an eminently readable and largely trust-worthy account of the causes, course and results of the Persian Wars. Enough documents were not available to him to write this book.

"In ancient Greece, history was transmitted orally and Herodotus himself must have read from history to auditors in Athens and Thurii. Though there were written materials in Persia, he could not read the languages. Therefore he gathered testimony from survivors and descendants of survivors of an era whose events he was too young to have experienced. But Herodotus had overcome these difficulties". Herodotus weighed and took possible and probable events for writing his history.

According to some critics his work is charged with credulity. "His work does not satisfy our notion of a critical history. But his descriptions of what actually happened in battles are usually lucid and convincing and they are embolished by accounts of individual valour in the Homeric tradition". This is given by Stephen Usher in "The Historians of Greece and Rome".

No doubt the history of 'Persian Wars' was written with purpose and passion. According to Herodotus, the Athenians were saviours of Greece.

The Persian Wars lasted for 25 years. It started in 500 B.C. and ended in 479 B.C. He provides information about the rise of the Persian Empire under Cyrus. Added to this he gives a clear picture of the battles of Marathon and Salamis, with the destruction of the Persian fleet at Salamis. Greece was saved from destruction. According to Stephen Usher "The originality of Herodotus lies in the manner to which he incorporated the tractable elements from disparate poetic traditions in a prose medium and judiciously adapted them to a single contemporary theme-the confrontation of East and West".

The task of Herodotus is a formidable one. His debts to earlier and contemporary writers are manifold. In the opinion of H.E. Barnes, "The fame of Herodotus will endure as the first constructive artist in the field of historical writing, as the author of the earliest comprehensive historical work, as the first writer to imply that the task of the historian is to reconstruct the whole past life of man as one of the most absorbing story-tellers in the entire course of historical writing".

(ii) Thucydides (456-404 B.C.): Herodotus wrote the first real history, Thucydides gave it a new shape and dimensions. He could tell a story as well as Herodotus. Historians generally refer Thucydides as "the first truly critical historian of the world". He was an Athenian citizen. By birth he was an aristocrat. He received a good education. So he was made to serve in political and military affairs.

Thucydides was twenty five years old when the Peloponnesian war broke out in 431 B.C. In 414 B.C. he was elevated to the position of a general to command the Athenian forces in Thrace. The defeat of his own ruler caused his dismissal and banishment. As a result of this he made an extensive travel for about 20 years. This helped him to observe events and to devote himself to his History. He died in 404 B.C.

Thucydides wrote his 'History of the Peloponnesian Wars' after his extensive travel. This was completely a new idea. He sought to discover the truth as historian. Although he made a distinction between the superficial and the profound causes of the war — unlike Herodotus, he was not particularly concerned with them. "Not causes but lessons were his object".

Thucydides thought that his 'History' will be judged useful by those inquirers who desire an exact knowledge of the past as an aid to the interpretation of the future, which in the course of human things must resemble if does not reflect it". With this ultimate object in his mind Thucydides wrote a history entirely different from that of Herodotus". "Herodotus is expansive, Thucydides concentrates 'Herodotus engages in digressions'. Thucydides strictly limits his range of topics".

Besides, Thucydides gave more importance to the political aspect of history the epic struggle between democratic imperial Athens and oligarchic, militarist Sparta. Thus, Thucydides becomes the forerunner among historians of political history.

Thucydides gave more importance to politics because, he was under the belief that in understanding political events and their social and military consequences, he could grasp the essential elements in human behaviour, elements which accounted for what he saw as the cyclical movement of history. Thus he was able to make it clear between what was "essential" and "demonstrable". According to him, "The conclusions I have drawn from the proofs quoted may, I believe safely be relied on".

The monumental work of Thucydides "History of the Peloponnesian War" consists of eight books. The last seven books cover the first twenty years of the war (431-411 B.C). The first book is introductory. The following books give a graphic picture of the war:

(a) Book II takes us down to spring of the year 428.
(b) Book III covers the next three years' events down to spring 425.
(c) Book IV deals about the Spartan proposals for peace and rejection and also the capture of Pylos, Sphacteria and Cythera by Athens.
(d) Book V contains the operations that led to the death of Celon Brasidus and the conclusion of Peace of Nicias.
(e) Book VI and VII cover the years 415 to 413. From these two books we get an elaborate account about the Sicilian expedition from beginning to end.
(f) Book VIII deals about the renewed war and its continuation and finally its abrupt end.

He has given a good account of the war in a descriptive manner. In spite of his hard work he did not complete the work and stopped it in mid campaign in 411. Yet one is tempted to ask the questions that why did he stop so abruptly. "But on this point conjecture is useless".

Thucydides wrote his books on the basis of strict rules of admissible evidence. No doubt he treated his material critically and rationally. His historical work observe Peter Gey and G. J. Cavanough, "not an essay which is to win the applause of the moment, but a possession for all time". J.B. Bury says that "the work of Thucydides marks the longest and most decisive step that ever be taken by a single man towards making history what it is today".

(iii) Xenophon (430-354 B.C.): Xenophon was a great soldier and statesman. He was born in a middle class family at Athens. He was the first man to denounce the myths of Homer and Hesiod. Under his leadership 10,000 Greek mercenaries treaded through the rugged terrains of Asia Minor and joined the service of Sparta.

During his later years at Elis, Xenophon devoted himself to writing. He died in 354 B.C. at the time of Macedonian glory.

Xenophon's first and foremost work to be mentioned here is "Memorabilia". In this work he preserves the recollecting of his master Socrates. It has been compared to the work of Plato. It gives a clue to the readers regarding the social life of the ancient Greeks.

Xenophon's another work was "Anabasis". It is considered as one of the most absorbing and thrilling memoirs produced in Greek. It gives a vivid account of the military operations of Cyrus the younger.

Xenophon's another great work was the "Hellenica", a history of Greece from 411 B.C. It gives the history of the Peloponnesian war from where Thucydides left it. From this we get a detailed account of "the Athenian and Spartan naval manoeuvres that followed upon the events described by Thucydides at the end of his unfinished eighth book".

From Hellenica we know that the Persians were superiors in the West. This prompted Alexander the Great to march to the East.

In spite of all this, Xenophon does not find a fine place in the list of historians like Herodotus and Thucydides. But no one can question his brilliance in his presentation. But unlike the other great historians he did not enquire into the causes and to appreciate the results of events. Like the great Philosopher Socrates, he was prone to explain the developments in terms of the work of Almighty. For instance, he attributed the fall of Sparta to the work of God. Like others he had his defects, but he had his virtues also. We find all features in his works. So Stephen Usher in his "Historians of Greece and Rome" says that "Xenophon's talents are best suited for such themes (imperialism, autonomy pan-hellenism, nationalism etc.); and these themes become a permanent part of ancient historiography".

(iv) Polybius (198-125 B.C.): Polybius was an Achaean Greek. He was born in 198 B.C. His father was a leading statesman in the Achaean League. As a young man he played a prominent part in the Achaean League. In 168 B.C. he was taken as a hostage to Rome during the battle of Pydra.

In Rome Polybius entered into the household of Aemitius Paulas. Then he became an intimate friend of the young Scipio Aemitianus. For the next two decades he enjoyed a very high social life. He also had the opportunity to travel Italy, Gaul, Spain and Northern Africa.

Polybius wrote a laboured style but his concept of history was an attempt to objectively present the conflicting interest in society; he was superior to his predecessors. He treated the Greeks and the Romans equally. Polybius considered the question of the reliability of the sources as of permanent importance. He brought to his task considerable talents and experience. He knew directly many of the political and military leaders in Greece and Rome. He had travelled through the lands which were the scenes of his "Histories".

Xenophon in his "History" of 40 volumes stressed the importance to the expansion and constitutional development of the Roman Empire. Of the forty volumes only five are in possession now; still these enable us to have a clear idea about the entire work. From those forty volumes we get a clear picture of the Punic Wars, the narrative from the time when Romans crossed the sea from Italy in 164 B.C. and other events connected with Carthage and Greece. His account of the decline of the Hellas and the growth of the Roman Empire are very interesting.

Xenophon had also contributed towards the advancement of Historiography. He gave utmost importance to methodology. Hence, James T. Shotwell says that "Polybius's guiding principles of historical writing are the first and noblest statement of scientific ideals for the historian until the days of Ranke..... and give Polybius so high a place in the history of history......as long as history endures the ideals of Polybius will be an ...... inspiration and guide".

Character of Greek Historiography: Greeks were interested in man itself. It is clearly seen from the study of the development of Greek Historiography of Herodotus, Thucydides, Xenophon and Polybius. To put it briefly "it is humanistic".

R.G. Collingwood says that the Greek writers and historians believed that "whatever happens in history happens as a direct result of human will; that some one is directly responsible for it, to be praised or blamed according as it is a good thing or a bad".

Secondly the Greek historians raised history to the level of science. Their writings were made on the basis of enquiry, criticism and analysis.

Thirdly during their period, history was treated as self-revelatory.

It goes without saying that the Greeks took keen interest in the achievements of men. During their period great developments took place in the working of democracy, struggle among various cities for supremacy, spread of Hellenic civilisation and imperialism of Rome. No wonder all these provided vast material for writing.

J.W. Thomson says that "The Greeks wrote history of all characters of all dimensions. The history of men are things of great nations and small cities, universal annals and local chronicles, political, literary and military memoirs. There is nothing which they forgot or ignored; the Greeks first learnt the art of writing real history and perceived its purposes, its duties, its laws. The Greeks were the organisers of history as they were of science and of philosophy".

(B) ROME

(i) Livy,

(ii) Tacitus

(iii) Character of Roinan Historiography

(i) Titus Livius or Livy (59-17 A.D.): Livy occupies a prominent place among the historians of Rome. He was born at Padua in 59 B.C. Stephen Usher in his book "The Historians of Greece and Rome" says that "Biologically Livy is the most obscure of the great historians". Nothing is available about his life. We get some information about Livy from the account of St. Jerome.

Livy enjoyed the patronage of Augustus Caesar and others in Rome. He devoted his time in literary field. He died in Rome in 17 A.D.

Livy wrote a national history of Rome from the establishment of the city to that of the Empire. In the history of Rome, Livy set himself the task of "Tracing the history of the Roman people, from the foundation of the city". He traced the history of seven hundred years in a beautiful manner in this work. He gave importance to political lessons like Thucydides and Polybius.

No wonder that Livy was very much interested in his historical undertaking, to write of Rome than which, "there was never any state either greater or more moral or richer in good examples". His work was "patriotic, moral and hortatory."

Livy gave a clear picture of Rome from its foundation by 753 B.C. to the death of Drusus in 9 A.D. in his voluminous work. Due to his sudden death he could not proceed with his work upto the end of the reign of Emperor Augustus.

Livy's entire work was divided into 142 books. The entire work narrates some seven hundred and seventy years history of the Roman Empire. Of these books only thirty five are available in an unabridged form I-X and XXI-XLV.

'History of Rome' was the life work of Livy. To write this monumental work he consulted the existing histories that were available to him. At the same time he never failed to note and question the dubious evidence. His approach was humanistic. He was under the impression that history should indicate morals and teach civic virtues. His language was lucid.

As a historian Livy had some defects. We find certain anachronisms in his account. His inexperience of the world often led him to misinterpret political leaders and to misconstrue their actions. There are also some factual errors in his account. Further his work was filled with omens, and prodigies which gave religious tone to his writing.

In spite of its drawbacks, Livy's work was a brilliant one. James T. Shotwell says that "he carried the idea of the fated mission of Rome as the unifying centre of the civilised world back across the centuries of its obscurity and linked together past, present and future in one culminating perspective".

(ii) Cornalius Tacitus (56 — 120 A.D.): According to Peter Gey and G.J. Cavanaugh, "Tacitus was the greatest of the Roman historians and his works have taught us much of what we know of Rome in the first Christian century".

Tacitus was born in 56 A.D. He was an aristocrat by birth. In other words he belonged to an aristocratic family. He showed keen interest in military education in his early days. He was also trained in governmental service. In addition to this he studied public speaking and moral philosophy. Between 112-113 he was proconsul in the province of Asia. He died some years after the accession of Hadrian in 117 A.D.

One of the earliest works of Tacitus was a 'Dialogue on Oratory'. It was a laudatory biography of his father-in-law Agricola. His another work was 'Germanica'. It is the study of 'the origin, the geography, institutions and tribes of the Germans'.

Tacitus's greatest works, 'the Histories' and 'the Annals' appeared in 105 and 106 respectively.

The above two works gave a detailed description of the Roman History from 14 to 96 A.D.

Seventeen books are at our disposal among the histories.

The available books among the Annals are:

(a) The reign of Tiberius (14-37),

(b) The reign of Claudius (47-54) (last 7 years),

(c) The reign of Nero (54-66) (first 12 years)

In spite of his excellent historical writing, he suffered from certain technical flaws. For writing the above works, he mostly depended upon oral declarations, rumours and gossip. So his approach to the theme was defective. He stood for republican form of government. Hence he was bitter against the imperial system of the Roman Empire. Nevertheless his reputation as historian and the greatness of his achievement remains unshaken. Ronold Syme praises Tacitus as a brilliant and successful historian of Rome in the method of history.

Character of Roman Historiography: Rome produced eminent historians like Livy, Tacitus, Caesar, Sallust and Seutonius Tranquillus. Tranquillus wrote his brilliant work, "The Lives of the Ceasars". In this he did not arrange the events according to sequence.

Due to political writings, decline began in historical writing in the 2nd century A.D. Rhetorical method gained momentum in historical writing. Roman historiography was humanistic in its approach. Man was the central figure. Great attention was paid to the achievements of man by great historians and eminent writers. This is considered as the first characteristic of the Roman historiography.

Secondly they did not give much importance to divine agency since its function was limited.

Thirdly the Roman historiography stressed importance to contemporary or current events only.

Fourthly to Livy Rome was the heroine of his history. He was very much concerned about Rome.

R.G. Collingwood points out, "Rome is the agent whose actions he is describing". He illustrates the substantialitic principle with particular reference to Livy. He says Livy set his mind to the task of writing a history of Rome.

Finally the Roman historians were guided by political leaders and this led to their partisan end.

Thus they ultimately impaired the steady progress and standard of historical writing.

(C) CHURCH HISTORIANS

(i) Eusebius

(ii) St. Augustine (iii) Contributions made by the Church

(i) Eusebius: With the emergence of Christianity as a universal religion, the church historians developed a keen interest in historical developments. Many began to write on the history of the church, while others recorded the events of their own times as well as preserved the rare manuscripts of the classical works of Greece and Rome. Among the historians Eusebius was the most important one.

Eusebius was the Father of church history. He was born in 260 A.D. probably in the city of Caesarea in Palestine. Later on he entered priesthood. After some years of travel and imprisonment and threatened martyrdom during the days of Diocletian's persecution of Christians (303-313), he became bishop of Caesarea in 314 A.D. He was the closest friend of Emperor Constantine. He died in the year 340 A.D.

Eusebius wrote forty-six books. Only a small number of them are available to us. They are:

(a) Historia Ecclesiastica
(b) The Chronicle
(c) The Lives of the Martyrs of Palestine
(d) The Life of Constantine.

'The Historia Ecclesiastica' or 'the History of the Church' gives an account of the church upto 309 A.D. It was continued by the writers like Socrates and Theodoretus. According to one writer, "Eusebius's work was more a collection of documents than a historical narrative". He collected the connected documents pertinent to his 'history'.

Eusebius was critical in his approach. His church had weathered the storm. Christianity had been recognised by the Roman Empire. At this juncture Eusebius composed the History of the Church. According to James T. Shotwell, "It is a co-ordinated, sustained, critical and interpretative history of the church, which grows deeper and fuller as the subject advances".

Eusebius's contribution to historical chronology is 'The Chronicle' which gives a clear picture of all ancient kingdoms. Besides, his 'Chronological Canons' deal about the chronological tables. 'The Life of Constantine' and 'The Book of Martyrs' contain only unnecessary details.

(ii) St. Augustine: Augustine was a great church historian. He contributed very much to the church history. He was born in 354 A.D. in the Roman province of Numidia, North Africa. He received literary education during his boyhood. He studied the works of Cicero, Virgil, Terence and Varro. Then he came under the influence of St. Ambrose. His works are

(a) Confessions,
(b) The City of God,
(c) Encyclopaedia.

St. Augustine's autobiographical "Confessions" can be regarded as one among the classics of western literature.

St. Augustine's "The City of God" was magnificent philosophical history in which he expounded the meaning of history and Christianity.

In the "City of God", Augustine presented a powerful defence of the role of Christianity in the Roman Empire. As Peter Gey and G. J. Cavanaugh rightly observe, "He was not concerned with preserving the memory of great events, as was Herodotus. Nor did he see history as offering lessons for statesmen as Thucydides and Polybius. He did not seek to explain or to describe the greatness of Rome, as did Livy, or to recount her decline from republican virtue as did Tacitus. Nor did he attempt a history of Christianity and the church within the broad sweep of universal history, as did Eusebius".

St. Augustine viewed history as a struggle between good and evil. Hence he pointed out that the struggle between the two would end in the victory of City of God, an embodiment of Good over the city of Satan an embodiment of Evil. In other words St. Augustine in his "City of God" represented the historical process as a struggle between good and evil, virtue and vice and the divine and the demoniac. Hence, Herbert Butterfield says that, "With St. Augustine history became a specifically Christian drama".

St. Augustine believed in Providence. Moreover he firmly believed that the whole course of history is of Providential.

St. Augustine got the idea of historical approach from the Bible. It gave him the form and content necessary for historiographic purposes. Estimating his work "The City of God" Peter Gey and G.J. Cavanaugh observe thus: "Human history took on a new theme, a new meaning and a new direction with Augustine's "City of God" — a consumate achievement as a philosophy of history". He was undoubtedly among the first and greatest of the Catholics for the Christian West. As a great Catholic he completed his monumental history of the "City of God".

(iii) Contributions made by the Church: With the advent of Christianity, historical writing took a new turn. Eusebius, St. Augustine, Sevres of Gaul, Orosius of Spain, Venerable Bede and Joachin of Floris did a wonderful service to historiography.

Firstly the Christian historians viewed everything as part of eternity. Secondly the Greek and Roman historians had a particular view of history. They had special interest of their own country. Christian historians focussed in their writings that wherever people lived, all were equally involved in carrying out the will of God. As R.G. Collingwood rightly points out, "Christian universal history has undergone a Copemican revolution, whereby the very idea of such a centre of gravity is destroyed". Thirdly, Christian historians gave a theistic character and outlook to history. They believed in Providence. The duty of a historian was to explain the working of Providence. Fourthly, for all happenings 'Almighty' was responsible according to them. In this connection R.G. Collingwood observes, "All these elements, so familiar in modern historical thought, are totally absent from Graeco-Roman historiography and were consciously and laboriously worked out by the early Christians". Thus the four principles gave a new outlook to history.

Christian historiography suffered from two defects:

1. that it was written to a purpose and as part of that purpose paganism was discredited and 2. their chronology was based on theological and not secular assumptions. But their ecclesiastical histories were more dependable.

Church historians treated primarily of miracles and saints. This kind of historical writing is called Patristic historiography.

Thus the church made remarkable contributions to historiography.

14

Medieval Historiography

Patristic historiography was the most important aspect of historical writing, during the Middle Ages. At the same time a fair measure of secular historical writing also developed in the medieval period.

During the Middle Ages, the shift from Christian methodology to secular did not mean really an improvement; since many modern writers who were merely chroniclers retained all the defects of the Patristic tradition but were also deficient in scholarship which was the hallmark of the monks.

The Christian monks had a monopoly of historiography during the Middle Ages. Further the medieval historians were themselves a small elite group of scholars who wrote to inform or to please another small elite group of readers.

The transitional period from the decline of Rome to the end of Charlemagne represented the first half of the medieval period and the centuries from Charlemagne to the Renaissance stood for the second half of that period; and each had its distinctive characteristics.

During the earlier period Cassiodorus' 'History of the Goths', Procopius' 'The History of his own Times', Paulus Wamifridus' 'History of Lombards' etc., were considered as the best historical writings.

Many Annals and Chronicles came into existence during the later period. First they began as diaries and then they developed into well-organised chronicles. The word 'annals' means 'annual information' particularly the astronomical records determining the exact date of the Easter festival. T.F. Tout who has made a study of medieval chronicles observes that 'its object in general was not a piece of literary imposition but to fulfil a practical need, to apply information or to prove same case'. At the some time chronicles could give authentic information on contemporary happenings but not on past events — nor could they discriminate reliable evidence from unreliable sources.

The 'Anglo-Saxon chronicle' of the medieval period considered as the most famous chronicle in this respect. The 'chronicle of St. Albans' relates to the events from 1250 to 1422. The chronicle of Otto of Freissing and the 'Greater chronicle of Mathew Paris' are other important chronicles of this age. The 'chronicle of London' and the 'chronicle of Florence' belonged to the later middle ages. They deal about the histories of the age.

The Medieval Historians Sources were Scanty: the method of source and text criticism developed in recent times did not exist then; and the natural sciences and the social sciences had not grown their later day features then.

In short medieval historiography, was 'characterised by dogmatic interpretation, primitiveness of literary form and want of scientific method'. These defects ultimately were got rid of in Europe only by the beginning of the 19th century . But it cannot be denied that the medieval historians did a wonderful work of preserving the history of their period with then available sources. No wonder it is a great service to the future historians.

15

Modern Historiography

(i) Renaissance Period: A fresh reorientation of historical studies began to appear at the close of the Middle Ages. Truly speaking "a reaction began with the Renaissance which brought about secularization of thought". During this period when the Turks took Constantinople they did a signal service to European intellectual tradition. The Greek and Roman scholars fled to the Western countries. Wherever they went, they brought the literature of ancient Greece and Rome and brought out a new interest in classical learning. On of the main tasks of the Renaissance period was to bring about a fresh reorientation of historical studies. According to R.G. Collingwood with the outbreak of Renaissance, "a return was made to a humanistic view of history based on that of the ancients".

During this period historical thought once more placed man in the centre of its picture. According to R.G. Collingwood, "Man for the Renaissance historian was not as depicted by ancient philosophy, controlling his actions and creating his destiny by the work of his intellect, but man as depicted by Christian thought a creature of passion and impulse".

Italy was the homeland of Renaissance. It was hence called "School of Europe". Classical traditions were cherished and nourished in Italy. It paved the way for the rise of development of historical writing.

The historians of the Renaissance period displayed the essential qualities of a historian namely a critical spirit and an objective attitude. Among them Giavanni Villani, Leonardo Bruni and Coria were very important.

Villani wrote the 'History of Florence'. In this book he gave great importance to the causes, course and results of events. He made a clear distinction between Legend and history. Further he gave importance to human and psychological factors.

Coria wrote the 'History of Milan'. In this great historical work, he gave utmost importance to the social and economic factors.

(1) NICCOLO MACHIAVELLI (1469 — 1527)

Undoubtedly Niccolo Machiavelli was the greatest historian of the Renaissance period. He was the son of a Florentine judge. He read the Latin classics with great zeal and interest and came under the influence of Polybius. At the age of 25, he took up a position in the government. The fall of the Republic and restoration of the Medici led to his imprisonment and possibly torture. When Cardinal Medici became Pope Leo X, his release became possible. Then he returned to his villa where he died on 21st June 1527.

Machiavelli belonged to the Age of Humanism. He produced quite a number of works. They were

(i) The Prince,
(ii) Discourses on Livy,
(iii) The History of Florence and
(iv) The Art of War.

Machiavelli liberated politics from the medieval religious influence and gave a truly secular outlook. He wrote the 'History of Florence' in eight volumes. He was greatly influenced by the writings of Polybius and Livy. H.E. Barnes in his "A History of Historical Writing" says in the following words, "it is doubtful if any previous historian had exhibited such power in grasping the nature of historical causation in its political aspects or in presenting a clear picture of the process of political development". F. Schevil on the other hand states that "Machiavelli was not a historian". It was not a good statement. No doubt he fully understood the historical background of Italy and he devoted himself to the ideal of a united Italy. He was not unsympathetic towards the church and its officials for he considered them as the main problem to Italian unity. He liked to substitute a materialistic theory of causation to the old religious supernationalism.

Machiavelli's political and historical philosophies are reflected in his monumental work, "The Prince". N. Subramanian prefers to call it a work on the grammar of power. The idea reflected in his work can be useful to any country for all time. What Issac Newton contributed to science was done by Machiavelli to political thought.

Machiavelli's "The Prince" came to be regarded as a manual for princes. The political behaviour, manner of diplomacy, intrigues in the courts and the methods by which states were won — all these find place in that masterpiece.

In his 'Discourses' Machiavelli had contributed a series of essays on government.

Machiavelli was not in favour of theological interpretation. As a historian he was unfavourable to this idea. He wanted to find out the natural laws which governed the life of the people. In his 'The Art of War' he reveals his shrewd mind in analysing the techniques of war. Again he points out that a citizen soldiery would be useful in preserving liberty. Like the great historians, he attached importance to the causes and results of events.

As a realist, Machiavelli exposed the nature of power and people who were mad after power. For, 'Power corrupts man. Absolute power corrupts absolutely'. He pointed out that ends justify the means in one's pursuit towards any policy. His historical works however were not as important as his single slim book 'The Prince'.

Francesco Guicciardini (1483-1540)

He was a contemporary of Machiavelli. He wrote a History of Florence which is a more truly historical work. He avoided the philosophical comments and degressions so frequent in Machiavelli but concentrated on 'a vigorous and incisive narrative of events and a candid criticism of men and politics'. He was an impartial historian. Edward Futer says thus "with the Florentine history modern analytical historiography and political ratiocination in history began. He also wrote a 'History of Italy' which was the first general history of Italy. Guicciardini's work reached the highest level of historiography before the era of Camden and Clarendon.

The Renaissance spread to other countries of Europe from Italy. France came under the influence of Renaissance in Italy. Philippe a politician and a scholar contributed to the historical memoirs. Ganguin produced the history of France. Hugo Grotius a distinguished Dutch humanist historian (1583- 1645) wrote on the Goths, Vandals and Lombards. He took a secular view of history and pointed out that religious wars were the stumbling blocks to the natural development of the Netherlands. He was the leading historian among the many contributors to International Law.

Jean Bodin (1530-1596): Bodin took a keen interest in the methods of historical studies. He produced a scholarly work 'Method for easily understanding History'. It was the first elaborate work on Historical method with special reference to interpretation. He laid great stress on the influence of geography on history and thus anticipated Montesquieu and Buckle.

The Duke of St Simon (1675-1755): St. Simon wrote a brilliant account of France under the Bourbons. It was one of the most entertaining historical work ever written. "It was hypnotic in its influence" according to G.P. Gooch.

Thus this brought the Humanist period to an end.

(ii) Reformation Period: When Machiavelli was planning to write the History of Florence, Martin Luther was burning the Papal Bull at Wittenburg and bringing about the Protestant Revolution. Later it led to Counter-Reformation. In many European countries like Germany and England people studied the classical literature with great interest and enthusiasm. Reformation created an abiding interest to historical writings more than Renaissance. A number of scholars and writers made an attempt to produce historical works. There is no critical analysis in the works. They developed a biased attitude towards protestant religion which tarnished their writings.

Sebastian Frank wrote a book on world history, attaching importance to social conditions during this period.

John Carien's 'Chronicle' provided a historical sketch from Adam to 1532 A.D.

Flacius wrote his 'Centuries'. He treated history as a struggle between God and Evil, pointing out that virtue will triumph over vice in the end. From this work we know that everything happens in this world according to Divine Plan and the 'Almighty' was the central figure of history.

Sir Thomas More wrote History of Richard III, George Cavendish produced an equally scholarly work on the 'Life of Cardinal Wolsey'. Sir Walter Raleigh's 'History of the World' was a remarkable work. Francis Bacon's Henry VII urged the necessity of a scientific study of history, based upon an examination of facts. Thomas Hobbes, a political thinker in his 'Social Contract' says that monarchy was largely responsible for the growth of secular and scientific history.

The autobiography of Ignatius Loyola who founded the Jesuit Order was a confession of his faith and the result of honest introspection.

Niccolo Orlandini's 'History of the Society of Jesus' is a good example of conscientious historiography on the part of a man of religion.

Belgian Jesuits under the leadership of Jean Boland (1596-1665) started collecting the lives of the saints under the heading 'The Acta Sanctorum'.

Bishop Burnet's 'History of the Reformation of the Church of England' was a good account of the Reformation Movement in many of its aspects.

The Ecclesiastical Annals of Bamius in 12 volumes was a reply in kind to the attack of Papacy by Flacius in his 'Centuries'.

Thus Reformation and Counter-Reformation made use of history as a tool for propaganda and not as a value in itself.

(iii) Cartesianism and Anti-Cartesianism: The Intellectual Revolution was inaugurated by Rane Descartes, Sir Issac Newton and John Locke in Europe during the 18th century. The ideas and principles advocated by Rane Descartes contributed to cartesianism.

Rane Descartes: Rane Descartes was a French Philosopher. His famous work was "Discourse on Method".

Rane Descartes was a great soldier and mathematician. He was also a physicist. Later he became an advocate. He disliked the existing forms of government. He had no faith in the use of books. He advocated reason as the only path to knowledge. His writings were severely attacked by the other writers of his period. It endangered his life. So he fled from his country and took asylum in Holland.

The foremost conception of Rane Descartes was the mechanistic universe. According to him every individual thing, whether it was the solar system, the earth or the moon, everything is a self operating machine. This is mainly due to a force rising from the original motion provided by the Almighty to the universe. This general mechanistic pattern is seen both in animals and human beings. Man is different from animals because of his reasoning power.

Though Descartes disliked history, his principles are favourable to history. They are applied history. He put great stress that the natural world was mechanically constituted and he believed that general laws could be applied to nature. Since man being a product of nature, he is also controlled by natural laws.

Thus one finds that Cartesian historiography subjecting history to systematic scepticism.

Many writers began to apply the cartesian principles in their historical works. The first of such type was Pierre Bayle of France. He attacked the Catholic interpretation of the Bible. He also derecognised the classical literature of the Pagans as extraordinary works.

Another writer was Titlement. He wrote "History of the Roman Emperors".

The Bollandists a school of Benedictine scholars made a critical study of the sources and rewrote the lives of the saints.

John Harsley made the first systematic collection of the Roman inscriptions in Britain.

(2) MONTESQUIEU

Montesquieu (1689-1755) was a French philosophical historian. He also applied cartesian principles to history. His works were the "Spirit of Laws", "Persian Letters" and the "Considerations". His "Spirit of Laws" published in 1748 displays a scientific treatment of the social and political phenomena. He was dissatisfied with all forms of government. He came to believe that despotism is best suited for countries with vast area, limited monarchy for small area and republican government for states with very small area.

According to Montesquieu there are three divisions in the government *viz.*, legislative, executive and the judiciary. They should be kept separate as water tight compartments. There should be separation of powers, otherwise there would be tyranny. This great idea of Montesquieu was accepted by France and the United States of America. It was incorporated in their respective constitutions.

Montesquieu's main historical work was the "Causes of the Greatness and the Decadence of the Romans". It ably interpreted the fact that Roman imperial decline was caused by its excessive territorial expansion which taxed its country too much. He was ever, more of a political philosopher and a sociologist than a historian.

Besides, Montesquieu also dealt with other matters. He believed that the nature of institutions is given shape by the physical environment. Montesquieu along with other historians discarded the theological interpretations and paved the way for a scientific history of human culture. Yet in certain other respects he differed from other writers. "History conceived by him was a kind of natural history of man". According to him the differences between nations and cultures are due to climate and geography. For all these reasons human reason is highly responsible according to Montesquieu.

Montesquieu was one of the basic causes for the intellectual unrest which made the French Revolution possible in 1789.

Ante-Cartesianism: Vico: Giovanni Battista Vico (1668-1744), the Italian jurist made significant contribution to the theory of history. He was a Neo-politan.

Vico was the son of a book-seller in Naples, Italy. He got himself well-versed in history, literature, philosophy and law early in his life.

Vico became professor of rhetoric at the university of Naples in 1689. He was influenced by Plato, Tacitus, Bacon and Grotius. "From Plato he learned method of approach, from Tacitus an appreciation of historical facts, from Bacon the technique of investigation and from Grotius certain aspects of universal law in history".

Vico wrote the "Scienza Neova" (New Science) in 1725. His next work was his "Autobiography". He totally rejected cartesianism. He did not neglect the importance of mathematical knowledge. But he was not prepared to accept the Cartesian philosophers' claim that no other kind of knowledge was possible.

According to Vico man erected his own history. He viewed historical process as a process by which man builds up his language, law, custom, manner and other things.

The Anti-cartesians viewed history thus: "History is not the story of quantitative but it is that of the development of societies and their institutions".

Vico thinks that from myths and traditions to modern scientific analysis there is a definite historical development. The general principles formulated by Vico are immensely useful in studying history, cites a few prejudices, against which the historians are to be alert and watchful always. While making reference about the source material, Vico indicates, the different branches of it like mythology and etymology, which can be utilised in finding out historical evidence.

(iv) Enlightenment: The age of intellectualism could be called the Age of Erudition or Rationalism or the Age of Enlightenment. The 18th century saw its flowering and passing. Rationalistic historiography was the result of both scientific discoveries and the geographical discoveries. It took place in Europe in the 18th century. The movement arrived at the secularisation of every aspect of life. Its philosophy is based upon the following concepts: "that reason is the only infallible guide to wisdom, that reason and instinct guide people to human perfectibility that the simplest and most natural structure of society is the best and that universe is a machine governed by inflexible laws which cannot be changed and that the order of nature is absolutely uniform and is not subject to any divine interference".

The real founders of the Enlightenment movement were Sir Issac Newton and John Locke. It was aided by the Philosophers like Descartes, Spinoza and Hobbes.

Vico, Hume and Turgot thought of an orderly development of human evolution on this earth in all its aspects, social as well as natural, Hobbes and Spinoza spearheaded a new historical enquiry by introducing Biblical criticism; the latter maintained that the old Testament must be treated like any other historical text.

David Hume, Adam Smith, Voltaire and Gibbon also belonged to the age of Enlightenment.

Among the British historical philosophers David Hume was the most popular and he made significant contribution to historical studies. Like Voltaire, he appreciated the importance of social relations, art, literature and morals for historical studies.

Adam Smith, produced his monumental work, "Wealth of Nations". He was under the belief that "the welfare of the society and wealth of the nation are best promoted when people pursue their own interests".

The writings of Voltaire, Montesquieu etc. gave definitely a new direction to European historiography. Voltaire (1694-1778) the noted French thinker criticised the nobles and officials of France. His works were "Philosophical Dictionary", "Utopia of El Dorado" and the "Essays". In the first work Voltaire advocated the doctrine that the world was governed by natural laws. The "Essays" gave an outline of world history which treated human history in all its manifestation like art, learning, science, custom, daily life and technology. From this work we also get an account of the Arabs, the Chinese and the Indians. Voltaire believed the ultimate triumph of reason in his "Essays".

The man who really influenced the Enlightenment Movement was Edward Gibbon. He held that the decline of the great Roman Empire signified the triumph of religion and barbarism. Thus the age of Enlightenment contributed much to historiography.

(v) Romantic Idealism: A new perspective to the study of the past was added in the second half of the 18th century. It was called Romantic Idealism. The fore-runner of this Romantic idealism was Rousseau. Though he was in the intellectual camp, he shared Voltaire's and Montesquieu's objection to the "Status quo" but behaved like a Romanticist in his general attitude, in spite of his being staunch opponent of despotism of all kinds. According to Collingwood, "the principle on which Rousseau explained history, therefore was a principle which would be applied not only to the recent history of the civilised world but to the history of all races and all times. Age of barbarism and superstition because at least in principle intelligible and it was possible to see the whole of human history, if not as the history of human reason, at least as the history of human will".

Among romantic historians apart from the immediate disciples of Rousseau, we can mention Madame de Stael who in her turn influenced Thomas Carlyle. The literary works of Sir Walter Scott were eminent products of this romantic Medievalism which did great service in that it dispelled effectively the prejudices of the Age of Enlightenment against the Middle Ages. Chateaubriand of France could be compared to Scott.

J.L. Motley, the American author of "Rise of the Dutch Republic" belongs to the above distinguished group of Romantic historians. The main achievement of the romanticist school was to have aroused unprecedented interest in nationalism among historians and to have held the field largely in the 19th century.

The romantic idealism inculcated the important ideas regarding the past. Further it correlated the events of the past to a natural explanation of progress and continuity. Of the important writers of the movement, mention may be made of Herder, Kant and Hegel.

(a) Herder: John Gottfried Von Herder (1744-1803) was one of the founders of the Philosophy of History. He was a German Professor in the above subject. He deals with the human past in the context of natural settings. Herder studied theology and was influenced by Kant in his early life though later on he was engaged in controversies with the great German philosopher.

Herder was interested in literature, art, language, religion and historical development. His major work on historical theory was the "Ident for the Philosophy of the History of humanity". He indicated the link between spiritual and natural worlds in his book. He summarises his views on history in the following manner:

(1) The end of human nature is humanity; they may realise their end; their fate is put in their hands by God.

(2) Contemplation of the past could lead to perfection in the future.

(3) To him civilisation unfolds as naturally as a flower; man fulfils himself by reaching the highest stature he is capable of.

(4) Even the very nature of human mind, reason and justice must gain more footing among man in the course of time and promote the extension of humanity.

(5) "A wise goodness disposes the fate of mankind", and therefore there is no nobler merit, no poorer or more abiding happiness, than to cooperate in its designs.

No wonder Herder stimulated thoughts of the subsequent writers on the problem of nature and mankind.

Herder's insight and originality were really commendable. In short he sought to explain the inherent differences among various races.

(b) Kant: Immanuel Kant (1724-1804) was the greatest German philosopher. He was born at Konigsburg. He was basically a student of theology, philosophy and mathematics.

In his famous analysis of Knowledge in the "Critique of Pure Reason" he was concerned more with scientific and mathematical knowledge.

Kant wrote a small pamphlet in 1784 on the idea of a "Universal History" from a cosmopolitan point of view. Therein he suggests a teleological principle according to which historical movements can be justified.

According to Kant, there were laws in nature obeyed by human beings and the study of the past might unearth the laws governing the conduct of human beings.

Kant believed that nature's plan was the development of human freedom. Collingwood beautifully sums up the argument of Kant in these words: "History then, is a progress towards rationality which is at the same time an advance of rationality...... The purpose of nature for the development of man's reason is a purpose that can be folly realised only in the history of the human race and not in an individual life".

Kant's theory of history was explained in his proposition "dealing with the social significance of the principle of antagonism". In this Connection H.E. Barnes too gives his opinion about Kant's theory of history. Kant stressed upon moral progress and believed in an order of world where states would eschew war and create ideal condition for moral advancement.

George Wilhelm Friedrich Hegel (1770-1831)

Hegel was born in Stuttgart in Wurtumberg in Southern Germany in 1770. His father was a civil servant. In his school days he was vary bright and brilliant and hence he became a school prize winner. Then he studied theology in the University of Tabingen. He fell under the spell of the French Revolution in his youth and declared it as "a glorious mental dawn". During this time he was very thorough with the writings of Rousseau. He worked as a private tutor for sometime. There he wrote the life of Jesus Christ.

In 1801 he became lecturer in the University of Jena. Now he came into contact with Kant.

Hegel wrote "The Phenomenology of Spirit", "Logic", "The Philosophy of Right" and "The Philosophy of History".

Hegel completed the work of Romanticism by inducting an idealism through his powerful weapon of dialectic. The path had been paved for Hegel by earlier thinkers to bring about a forceful argument for reconciling moral and natural order of things. G.H. Sabine in his "A History of Political Thought" says that "Hegel's Philosophy professed to offer an enlarged conception of reason that should overlap and include what had been separated by the analysis of Hume and Kant and the center of this system was a new logic purporting to systematize a new intellectual method. This he called dialectic". The French Revolution completely changed his outlook.

According to Sabine, "Hegel's dialectic in fact a kind of symbol for revolution and recovery....... The impersonal forces inherent in society itself work out their own destiny".

According to Hegel, the progress of human civilisation has not been in a positive straight line. It was in a zig-zag sort of movement. The aim of philosophy was to know nature and the entire works of experience and to comprehend the reason for it. The world is essentially dynamic and it is not static. The true concept must be an active moving process, a process of evolution. In the process of evolution, something that is undeveloped gets developed by splitting up, assuming many different and opposing forms. It then unites or combines again in a new concrete object and becomes a unity in diversity. The higher stage in the process of evolution is the realisation of the lower. The lower form is negatived in the higher. It gets carried over or sublimated. The whole process of evolution was given the name of Dialectic by Hegel. The term 'Dialectic' was first used by the sophists and other Greek thinkers.

According to Hegel the dialectic was a method or process by which all ideas in the world developed. History showed a continuous and orderly development. Hegel in and through his dialectic propounded the belief that reality could only be apprehended by a method of contrasting one thing with its opposite. Thus goodness was only understood when it was contrasted with badness, heat with cold, want with satiety. To Hegel the real was the rational and the rational was the real.

The universe of known experience was in constant flux. It was moving towards a definite point. It was governed by definite rational principles of 'Thesis' 'antithesis' and 'synthesis'. According to him abstract universal concept is called Thesis; the concept gives rise to contradiction called antithesis; the contradictory concepts are reconciled in the third called synthesis. It is the union of the other two concepts. There in the simple example of the evolution of the egg the whole dialectic process could be seen. The egg contains a germ (Thesis) which when fertilized gradually consumes (negatives) the contents of the egg. This act of destruction results not in death but the production of a new form of life completely different in nature from its origin the germ or its environment the contents. A chick (the synthesis of the two forces) emerges from the shell.

Hegel came for ward to demonstrate that the laws of thought were similar to the laws of the universe. The thesis "despotism" will call into being "democracy", the antithesis and from the clash between them the synthesis "constitutional monarchy" which contains the best of both results.

Further Hegel distinguished between understanding and reason as did Carlyle.

Hegel also emphasised the need of history and traditions to solve the political and other problems. "The History of the world" therefore says Hegel presents us with a rational process. The "Spirit" on the way to its goal makes many experiments. The spirit or the Reason does not know anything at the beginning of the world process. It develops slowly throughout the history of the world and ultimately reaches the truth — Absolute. Hence, it is called the rational is the real and the real is the rational.

From the above theory of Hegel it is seen that the main purpose of Dialectic is to display historical necessity. He used his theory for giving an explanation of the progress of society and its institutions. Hegel believed that nations were units in the universal order of things and individuals played their role in full subordination to the role of nation.

Thus Hegel's influence stimulated both philosophical and historical speculations in the succeeding period.

(vi) Utilitarianism: Jeremy Bentham was the founder of utilitarianism. He was born in London on Friday 15, 1748. His father was a lawyer. His father wanted his son also to be a lawyer. He showed great interest in Greek and Latin verses. Bentham was the chief promoter of the University College, London. His first and foremost disciple was James Mill.

Bantham was a great writer. He published as many as 30 works during his life time. Nearly 20 works were published posthumously.

The moral and political philosophy of Bentham is based on his doctrine of utility. In the "Fragment on Government" published in 1776 he preached the principle of the greatest happiness of the greatest number. The whole structure of his utilitarian theory rests on his assumption that "Nature has placed mankind under two sovereign masters pain and pleasure." To seek pleasure and avoid pain is the tendency of the human beings. Everything that brings happiness is good, he tells us and nothing that does not bring happiness is good.

According to Bentham pleasure and pain supplied the motive force to the activities of man. Every man tried to get pleasure and avoid pain. The doctrine of utility, therefore, is a hedonistic doctrine.

According to Bentham pleasure and pain depend upon the actions of the individuals. If their actions are right, they would promote happiness. If their actions are wrong, they would promote their unhappiness. He applies this to political science to promote the happiness of the community. It reflected in the 19th century legislations in England. Thus he was able to preach a message of humanism.

Bentham stands for free government on the basis of the principle of utility. He is in favour of unicameral legislature. All are equal before the eyes of law. He stands for equal distribution of wealth. These are the basic principles of the representative form of government.

J.S. Mill was also a great utilitarian. His writings profoundly influenced the later historians.

(vii) Positivism: According to Collingwood, 'Positivism may be defined as philosophy acting in the service of natural science as in the middle ages philosophy acted in the services of theology." But the positivists had their own notion of what natural science was. They thought that it consists of two things, first ascertaining facts, secondly, framing laws."

According to Positivists "the facts were immediately ascertained by sensuous perception. The laws were framed through generalising from these facts by induction. Under this influence a new kind of historiography arose, which may be called positivistic historiography." Even in Hume's ideas certain strains of utilitarianism and positivism can be discerned.

The positivists held that unless such laws were framed history could not be scientific. They contended that a vast accumulation of facts and systematic analysis would produce reasonable sets of Laws. The scientific approach would bring forth veritable Laws. Thus the study of history is very helpful.

The positivists had great faith in collecting historical datas and documents. The facts concerned about human activities. In their opinion such wide ranging facts would lead to clues for the discovery of facts.

R.G. Collingwood observes certain drawbacks in this approach.

Firstly the human past cannot be treated on par with scientific studies for obvious reasons. All the tests are possible in sciences; past events cannot be put in this type of investigation.

Secondly the historian cannot demonstrate the validity of his findings like that of a scientist.

Thirdly they failed to realise that historical events are unique though generalisations flow from particular details.

Finally the emphasis on analysis of innumerable events would result in overlooking the obvious general tendencies.

(viii) Scientific Socialism: Karl Marx is considered as the father of socialism. He was a great German Philosopher. He is the most important figure in the history of socialist thinking. He was born on May 5,1818 in the city of Traves in Prussia. His parents were Jews. He had his education at Bonn, Berlin and Jena. He studied history, philosophy and jurisprudence. His final ideas on history, economics and philosophy materialised during his studies in London. In Paris where he was working as a journalist, he contributed articles on Hegelian philosophy. In 1845 he was expelled from France and he retired to Brussels. There he organised the German Working Men's Association.

In 1848 on collaboration with Frederick Engels, he wrote "The Communist Manifesto". The book gives a clear idea of Marx's whole social philosophy.

In his philosophy of history Marx laid down the principles that social relationships depend upon modes of production and that the principles and categories thus created merely express historical and transitory situations. The Manifesto of the Communist Party tried to prove that the Industrial Revolution had made feudal conditions obsolete and concluded with the resounding words, "The workers have nothing to lose but their chains. They have the world to win; workers of the world, unite."

In 1859 Karl Marx spent much of his time in British museum collecting material for his classic that was to come Das Capital the first volume of which was published in 1857 and the third in 1894 under the editorship of Engels, it is the most famous book on socialism. It is considered as the Bible of the socialists. His other works are:

(i) A contribution to the critique of Political Economy.

(ii) 'Value, Price and Profit'.

(iii) 'Poverty of Philosophy'.

Karl Marx died on 14th March 1883.

Marx did not specifically write on historical problems. His general account of the materialistic concept of history is found in a few pages of the introduction to his critique of political economy. He says that the historical process is determined by the economic background. To him the history of all societies is the history of class struggles. Marx borrowed the idea of dialectics from Hegel and said that human history falls into phases distinguishable by different forms of social organisation and which are replaced successively by a dialectical process.

Marx's influence has been tremendous in the second half of the 19th and the first half of the 20th centuries, for his argument was valid upto the then state of industrial society. It is losing its formation when it has been proved that welfarism is possible by side tracking the class-struggles. A major defeat in the Marxian thought on the historical process is that when the classless communist society is achieved, the dialectical process comes to dead end. But theoretically it cannot do so. Marx by outlining the development of human society from the state of slavery to that of socialism through feudalism and capitalism emphasises this development as inevitable and automatically becomes a determinist. Spenglar however did not give a remedy and Toynbee put his hopes in God's grace. Marx stresses the logic of history which is bound to take all societies to a communist heaven.

Marx rejected the notion that history can be explained with reference to any spiritual process. His labour theory of value makes great strides in this field. According to Marx the class struggle at present could be between the Bourgeoisie and the proletariat. The overthrow of the former by the latter results in the dictatorship of the proletariat, which incidentally Marx approves of.

Dialectical Materialism: Karl Marx was a prolific writer. In his writings he has given a beautiful sketch about the dialectical materialism. It is the principal element in Marxism. He borrowed the idea of dialectic from Hegel. But he applied the same for a different purpose.

In the dialectical method, Marx never mentioned what he meant by materialism. But he made it clear that his materialism was dialectical and not mechanical. In mechanical materialism evolution is the path taken by material things under the pressure of their environment. In dialectical materialism, evolution is the development of matter from within environment helping or hindering, but neither originating the evolutionary process nor capable of preventing it from reaching its inevitable goal. Marx wanted to change the world *i.e.*, wanted to change for the better world by applying this principle.

According to Marx the dialectical principle is of universal application in as much as all development is the "struggle of opposites" or "conflict of opposites". Each stage reached in the march to the classless society, thesis, calls into being its opposite or anti-thesis and from the clash between the two a new synthesis emerges. The same process would continue till the perfect goal has been achieved. Marx defines dialectics at "the science of the general laws of motion, both of the external world and of human thought". Thus Marx believes in historical materialism on the one hand and dialectical materialism on the other.

From the above facts it is quite clear that Marx had followed very closely the ideas of Hegel. According to C.L. Wayper, "For Hegel the universal substance was Spirit; for Marx it was Matter. Both Spirit and Matter need to develop themselves and both do so by means of an inner dialectic. For Hegel the inevitable goal was the idea fully conscious of itself; for Marx the goal was the classless society, perfectly organised for production, sufficient for itself." In this connection Lenin had beautifully remarked that it is very difficult to understand Marx without reading Hegel.

In the Communist Manifesto the necessity for the dialectical process is argued in a vivid manner. In it Marx shows that human societies have developed dialectically because of the interaction between the continually changing methods by which men have performed the most essential business of their lives. It is seen from the dialectics that no system is permanent. As a result of every historically developed social form is in fluid movement. To put it in a nutshell the dialectical principle *viz.*, thesis, anti-thesis, synthesis is applied to social struggle between the bourgeoisie (thesis) the proletariat (anti-thesis), leading to the classless society (negation of negation synthesis). In this way the principle of dialectism is related to the ultimate break down of the capitalist system.

According to Marx all history is a history of class conflict. The conflict and confrontation between the bourgeoisie and the proletariat is relentless and in this struggle that dialectical principle shows that bourgeoisie will go under and the exploiters shall be exploited. Consequently the entire structure of society will be transformed.

According to Marx, two contradictions faced each other in society. Capital was the thesis and labour was its anti-thesis. Under the circumstance what was the synthesis? According to Marx capital had completed its cycle of evolution. It was dissolving. In the circumstances stated above capital had developed the technique of large scale production to perfection. It had fulfilled an important function of transforming individual labour process into "a combined social labour process." It paved the way for the increase of capital and the increase of workers. Now arose the conflict between the exploiter and the exploited, for production and protection they had to cooperate with each other. Thereby they decided to achieve restricted hours of work, uniform wage and uniform working days. In the evolution of society social control followed closely upon the heals of capitalism.

According to Sabine, "the history of human civilisation is a succession of national cultures in which each nation brings its particular and timely contribution to the whole human achievement". As Marx wrote in the preface to the second edition of "Das Capital", "in Hegel's writings, dialectic stands on its head. You must turn it right way up again if you want to discover the rational kernel that is hidden away within the wrappings of mystification."

16

Western Historians

(1) Machiavelli (Refer Chapter 15)

(2) Montesquieu (Refer Chapter 15)

(3) Voltaire

The founder of the Rationalist school of historians was Francis Arouet, popularly known as Voltaire (1694-1778). He was a French Philosopher. He was born on November 21,1694. He was very fond of literature. Like Montesquieu, Voltaire also admired the contemporary English civilisation and he was a fearless critic whose biting satire and keen wit chose for their special victim the established Roman Church.

Voltaire was an essayist, novelist, critic and historian. "History of Charles XII" and "Philosophical Letters" were published by him in 1731 and 1734 respectively. Charles XII of Sweden was his earliest attempt at historiography. It was excellent as a piece of literature. It was fit to inaugurate the Enlightenment era, though his later works were greater. 'Brevity, precision, lucidity characterise his writings. And the result is that the person of Charles XII stands out from the text as if he had been etched on steel' says a critic. Voltaire's 'The Age of Louis XIV' is the most polished of his works. It has been called 'the first modern historical work'. The civilisation of France and its greatest king are described adequately and satisfactorily. His 'Essay on the Manners and Spirit of the Nations' was a sort of universal cultural history. It was the real foundation of the history of civilisation in the Modern sense. Voltaire gave currency to the expression 'Philosophy of History'. The era of Enlightenment in historiography produced such eminent historians like David Hume, William Robertson and Edward Gibbon besides Voltaire.

Voltaire's main target of attack was the Roman Catholic Church. He condemned organised Christianity for his basic belief in the supernatural and for what he held to be its support of social justice. Hence, he was of the opinion that the middle ages was a period of barbarous misery. He hated the Jews for their begotten Christianity. In his 'Treatise on Toleration' he writes that "a fanaticism composed of superstition and ignorance has been the sickness of all the centuries".

Voltaire had firm belief in historical cycles. He had good hopes of four cultural events like Periclean Athens, Augustian Rome, Renaissance Italy and France under Louis XTV. But he had great devotion to Enlightenment. His famous saying that, "If God did not exist, it would be necessary to invent him", has often been misinterpreted as to stamp him as an atheist. He not only attacked atheism but also orthodoxy in his works.

Voltaire was a radical in religious matters; but he was a conservative in the matters of politics. Theoretically he stands for republic. He considers that "men are rarely worthy to govern themselves." According to him monarchy was the most permanent and fittest form of government. That monarchy would be in absolute power. He was for drastic administrative and legal reforms. Moreover his writings along with the Rousseau greatly influenced the French People during the French Revolution.

(4) Rousseau

Rousseau was born of a poor family in Geneva on June 28, 1712. He lost his mother when he was very young. Since his father was a watch maker and a dancer, he was not able to give proper education to his son. Rousseau gained a general literary reputation in 1749. His famous book was "Social Contract". It was published in 1762. It was considered as the Bible of the French Revolution. It is a famous classic. He was a combination of intellectualist who shared the views of the Enlightenment and stood also at the threshold of Romanticism. Since he was a firm believer in the noble savage and his views on pre-contract man were quite romantic. He himself wrote little directly by way of history but his thoughts and writings influenced thinkers in many countries.

According to Bergson, "His (Rousseau's) was the most powerful of the influences which the human mind has experienced since Descartes." His influence greatly affected the mind of the world on par with other men. C.L. Wayper says that he left the stamp of his strong and original genius on politics, education, religion, literature, and it is hardly an exaggeration to say with Langson that he is to be found at the entrance to all the paths, leading to the present. He has earned a very good name and fame by his monumental work 'Social Contract'.

(5) Vico (Refer Chapter 15)

(6) Gibbon

Edward Gibbon (1734-1794) was the most popular and nationalist historian of England. He was born at Putney on 27th April 1737. He was the eldest son of seven children to Edward Gibbon and Julia Porten. His aunt Catherine Porten showed great interest on him. He was put to school at Westminster and he later entered Magdalen College, Oxford. But Oxford completely failed him. Unable to find consolation in the church of England he took refuge in the church of Rome.

His father sent him away to Lausanne where he studied French and particularly Voltaire. Ultimately it was Voltaire who drew Gibbon away from the Roman Church. He fell in love with Suzanne Cuxchod, daughter of a protestant pastor. His father vetoed the marriage proposal.

In April 1758 Gibbon returned from Lausanne. A few years later he joined the Hamshire militia. He never learnt the Greek language till the age of 24, though he had already become a great Latin scholar. His great mission in life was to write history. He did not know what history it was to be. He visited Rome in 1764.

Then he returned to England. In 1774 he entered parliament. He supported Lord North as a Parliamentarian. However his political career was not a successful one. In 1768 he decided to write "the tale of a city (Rome) which swelled into an empire", and took the literary world by storm. The entire work was published in England in April 1788. Soon his health declined largely because of neglect. He died in London in 1794. Gibbon never married, reminding us of Hobbes and Locke and again of Macaulay.

'The Decline and Fall' is such a perfect piece of historical composition that it has been admired greatly and declared the historian's craft at its best But still he has had his denigration in his own times and in the succeeding generations. 'The History of the Decline and Fall of the Roman Empire' was noted for painstaking research, accurate facts, brilliant arrangement and a fascinating style. The work appeared in 6 volumes. The first four volumes deal with the period from 180 A.D. to 641 A.D. in details, and volumes 5 and 6 provide only summary sketch for the period from 641 A.D. to 1453 A.D. "Three editions of the work" were quickly sold out Further instalments of the history were eagerly and anxiously awaited.

Even this great scholar had critics then as well as now. The main points of criticism levelled against his work were: 1. that he was unfair in his treatment of the history of Christianity and 2. that he had no sympathy with the very theme of his history, namely, the Byzantine empire.

In regard to the first criticism it may be pointed out that Gibbon's rationalism and his temperamental objection to writing enthusiastic history prevented his taking a view of Christianity which men of religion think it natural and proper to take. Moreover by nature he was insensitive to religious feelings.

Regarding the second point of criticism it is said that it is invalid since Gibbon had his rights to treat the subject as he pleased in so far as he did not distort facts. Gibbon laid emphasis more upon military and political developments and did not appreciate the importance of social forces and economic influences which shaped the historical developments.

Gibbon was convinced about the incorrigibility of mankind. He thought that History "is indeed little more than the register of the crimes, follies and misfortunes of mankind". "But it must be remembered that he was the child of his age, an age marked by enlightenment, scepticism and disillusion."

Glorious and glowing tributes have been paid by many writers like Frederick Harrison Black and Trevelyan to Gibbon's monumental work. H.E. Barnes pays a tribute to Gibbon's industry and scholarship and says that, "over a century and a half since his work appeared it is still highly regarded by scholars and is today perhaps the best and certainly the most realistic, general survey of the broad field he covered." The Cambridge History of English Literature pays, deserving tribute and says 'The Decline and Fall' is not only the greatest historical work in the English language, it is perhaps the greatest piece of Literary architecture "in any language."

Thus Gibbon did a wonderful service to historical writings.

(7) Kant (Refer Chapter 15)

(8) Hegel (Refer Chapter 15)

(9) J.S. Mill

J.S. Mill (1806-1873). John Stuart Mill is the most widely known 19th century British political writer. He was the last of the utilitarians and the foremost of the individualists. He was the eldest son of James Mill. He was born in London on May 10, 1806. He learnt Greek at the age of three. At eight he began to study Latin. He studied Greek and Latin classics which included those of Plato, Herodotus, Xenophan, Thucydides, Homer and Polybius. He studied political economy, particularly Adam Smith and David Ricardo. His father was his teacher and constant companion.

J.S. Mill was appointed to a clerical post in the East India Company in ,1823 and became head of his department in 1856. At the age of 59, he entered Parliament and sat there from 1865 to 1868. During his life time he wrote the following books:

(a) System of Logic.

(b) Principle of Political Economy.

(c) Considerations on Representative Government.

(d) Utilitarianism.

(e) The Subjection Women.

(f) Autobiography.

(g) Three Essays on Religion.

(h) On Liberty.

J.S. Mill wrote one of the earliesf of the Histories of India. He was a great friend of Carlyle and he had read Guizot and Michelet. He said that understanding a social phenomenon, was impossible merely on the basis of historical facts.

J.S. Mill decided to modify some of the basic tenets of utilitarianism to defend the same from the anti hedonist movement led by Carlyle. He opined that some pleasures are of a higher quality than others. J.S. Mill approved of Hamboldt's doctrine of "self-realisation".

J.S. Mill in his most famous essay "On Liberty" has given veiy valuable and significant views about individualism and laissez-faire. He was a powerful defender of individual liberty. There should not be any interference by the government in the affairs of the individual.

According to J.S. Mill the best form of government is representative government.

J.S. Mill has thus given his thoughts on historical writings to the succeeding generations in an excellent manner.

(10) Compte

Auguste Compte (1798-1857) was a French Philosopher. He was born in 1798 in Montbellier. He was trained as a mathematician. From his early life he was deeply interested in philosophical ideas. His most famous book was 'Course of Positive Philosophy.' It was written in 6 volumes. His another work was 'The System of Positive Polity.'

The single design of history as concerned by Compte is the progress of the human mind; and if the progress of human mind gives unity to the entire history of society, it is because according to Compte the same way of thinking must prevail in all realms of thought. Compte observed that the positivist method was indispensable in the sciences of his day. He was the inventor of the word sociology".

Auguste Compte states that history as a whole is essentially the development of the human mind. He describes the three stages of human thinking in the work. Thus Compte the founder of modern sociology contributed much to the historical writings.

(11) Marx (Refer Chapter 15)

(12) Ranke

Leopold Von Ranke (1735-1886) is the best known historian since Gibbon and is the greatest historian Germany has produced, not excepting Moumsen. At the university he studied philosophy and theology. After his educational career, he developed taste for history. He was an ardent student of Scott who amused him for a while but later irritated him by his 'factual inaccuracies'. Ranke detached himself from bias. He said that general historians and secondary sources are undependable and so archival and other original documents must be used and indicated. He wrote the History of Germany, England, Prussia, France, histories of war, biographies etc. His complete works comprise 54 in number.

The best known work of Ranke is his 'History of the Popes'. 'It was not only a great achievement of historical research but a work of art.' The first volume of this work was published in 1834 and the second and third in 1836. Ranke traced the development of papacy through the Middle Ages and pointed out that it was a great unifier of European civilisation. In the words of G.P. Gooch, "This work for the first time revealed his resources of research and judgement, narrative and portraiture. It combined spaciousness with a mastery of detail, a faculty of generalisation with minute accuracy." In 1880 when he was 85 years old, he published 'Universal History.' The world was astounded at the audacity of an octogenarian sitting down to such a task" (G.P. Gooch). Seven volumes were published before he died in May 1886 and the rest of the work was completed by his students and followers. Some of his last dictated works are a justification of Carlyle.

G.P. Gooch sums Ranke's services to history as follows:

(1) "he divorced the study of the past as much as humanly possible from the passions of the present, and tried to describe how things were as wie es eigentlich gewesen:
(2) he stressed the necessity of founding historical construction on strictly contemporary sources:
(3) he founded the science of writing history by the analysis of authorities contemporary or otherwise, in the light of the author's temperament, afflictions and opportunity of knowledge and by comparison with the testimony of other writers." "He was the greatest historical writer of modern times.... he remains the master of us all." But Edward Meyer severely criticised Ranke's 'Universal History'. He said, "Ranke lacked real preparation for his task. He had only occupied himself with antiquity in his youth. Yet felt himself justified in virtually ignoring the scientific work of half a century. Under such circumstances the attempt could only issue us total failure."

Another criticism levelled against him was that he was profoundly biased.

J.W. Thompson and B. J. Holm criticise Ranke. But he was not unrealistic in his call for objectivity. He said, "Don't bring up the argument that it is not possible to be objective. It is a known fact ...... but try to be more objective." In the opinion of N. Subramanian, "It was Ranke's privilege to have made history an autonomous discipline."

(13) Spengler

Oswald Spengler (1880-1936) made significant contribution to the study of history. He was born in 1880 at Blackenburg. He was the son of a postal official. He studied mathematics, philosophy and history at the universities of Munich, Berlin and Haile, and took to school teaching. In 1911 he left school teaching and devoted his time to writing. He completed the first draft of the 'Decline of the West' in 1914. The first volume appeared in 1917 and the second in 1922. He spoke destiny versus casualty and culture versus civilisation with a preference to former in both cases. His work is theoretically and highly pretentious. In his work appears the theme of continual emergence and dissolution of different cultures. This is a kind of circular, spiral or wave theory of rise and fall. He has great contempt for the traditional division of history into ancient, medieval and modern.

Spengler's fame as a philosopher historian rests entirely upon his 'Decline of the West' which is nothing but a study in the history of philosophy. According to him, "Each culture begins with the barbarism of a primitive society. It proceeds to develop a political organisation, arts and sciences, first in an archaic manner, then blossoming into its classical period, subsequently dwindling into decadence and finally sinking into new type of barbarism. Thus its life ends."

Spengler lists cultures which have already emerged in the history. They were:

(1) Egyptian (3400-1205 B.C.)
(2) Indian (1500-1400 B.C.)
(3) Chinese (1300-200 B.C.)
(4) Classical (1100-400 B.C.)
(5) Byzantine (300-1250 A.D)
(6) Mayan (600-960 B.C.)
(7) Arabian (300-1250 A.D.)
(8) Aztec (1325-1500 A.D.)
(9) Western

Spengler points out that each of these civilisations passed through a cycle of four distinct periods *viz.*, Spring, Summer, Autumn and Winter. The western civilisation according to Spengler was passing through the last phase *viz.*, winter. With the debacle of western civilisation, a new cycle is about to begin.

Spengler's cyclical theory came into severe criticism at the hands of R.I. Mohan (Philosophy of History). He has pointed out certain defects in his theory like distorted and inadequate knowledge of Eastern Culture.

Besides 'Decline of the West' Spengler wrote 'Man and Technics' and 'How of Decision'. But he has earned a very good name and fame as a philosopher historian only by his first book. Thus he did wonderful contribution to Historiography.

(14) Croce

Benedatto Croce (1886-1952): Croce, Italian philosopher, and critic, is the most important name among modern European historical theorists. His early life was not a happy one. Later in his life, he engaged himself in research in local history and antiquities and contributed articles and wrote books. The most noteworthy contribution made by him was 'The Philosophy of the Spirit', divided into four volumes.

Croce was an art critic, historical theorist and fastidious student of Italian culture. His style like that of Dilthy was obscure and even crude. His historical theory is based upon the idealistic conception of history. History for him is the creation of the present not an account of the past, history is the highest form of philosophy. To him nothing exist except the mind; an historical account will be the philosophical because it will be the present interpreting the past.

Croce distinguished history from that of science and advocated that history resembles art rather than science. The artist and the historian perceived the unique and the particular. To Croce scientific propositions are neither true nor false but merely useful. According to him all true knowledge is historical knowledge. To Croce all history is contemporary history. That is to say while the historian thinks of the past, that past event is contemporary with the act of thinking. Contemporaneity of history is achieved the moment a person takes interest in the event.

Croce did not like to formulate historical theories which attempted to portray history as a scheme moving towards a planned goal or as conforming to a casually determined scheme. He called such theories the philosophy of history.

(15) Beard

Charles Austin Beard (1874-1948): The most popular of the historians of the post-world war U.S.A. was undoubtedly Charles Austin Beard.

Charles Austin Beard was born at Knightstown in Louisiana (U.S.A.). He had his education at the universities of the De Pauw, Oxford, Cornell and Columbia. From 1907 to 1917, Beard worked as Professor of Politics when he resigned the post on the issue of academic freedom. Then he served as the director of a training school at New York. After that he began to write books on politics. The chief works of Beard were:

(a) American Government and Politics,

(b) The supreme court and the constitution,

(c) Economic origins of Jeffersonian Democracy,

(d) The Rise of American Civilisation,
(e) The Idea of National Interest,
(f) An Analytical study in American Foreign Policy,
(g) The American Spirit,
(h) America in Midpassage,
(i) The Republic,
(j) President Roosevelt and the coming of the war, 1941.

As pointed out by Harvay, Beard's contribution to historiography cannot be minimised or underestimated.

(16) Macaulay

Thomas Babington Macaulay (1800-1858) was a great politician, orator, essayist, critic, poet and above all historian. He was born at Rothley Temple, Leicestershire on 25th October 1800. He was the son of Zachary Macaulay, the famous proponent of the anti-slavery movement.

Macaulay was endowed with natural qualities which gave him tremendous advantage in life. His memory was unsurpassed and as G.P. Gooch says "It was as difficult for him to forget as for other people to remember". He once remarked that if every copy of "Paradise Lost", "The Pilgrims Progress" or Sir Charles Grandison were destroyed, he could reproduce them from recollection". But this was not his only gift. Of greater use than this dubious gift memory was his capacity for expression. His diction has earned a unique place in the history of English prose and young students aspiring to artistic expression read avidly not only his verses but memorised his passages and took pride in reciting them. The style is his own, to be admired and not to be imitated.

When he was eight years old he wrote a 'Universal History' which is unimaginable by anybody in the world. He read all kinds of books. In 'The Lays of Ancient Rome' he portrays the graphic picture of Rome. His famous 'Essay on Milton' indicated his dazzling brilliance of the language introduced by him.

In 1830 he entered Parliament. Then he served as a Member in Governor General's Council during the time of Lord William Bentinck. After that he became Paymaster-General in England.

From the very beginning he was considered to be the historian of England. Ever since he returned from England he had been contemplating a History of England from the Restoration to the death of George IV and in 1839 he started writing. He was deeply involved in writing history and so he declined the honour of professorship of Modern History of Cambridge. The first two volumes came out in 1848. Then he began to complete the 'Magnum Opus'. The book went into translation into most of the European languages. Many writers praised the book in those days. It was considered as one of the finest pieces of historical literature in the English language. In this matter he stood shoulder to shoulder with Gibbon. Moreover this same method was carried out by Carlyle, Froude and Trevelyan in the subsequent years. In his history he tells the story of England in a beautiful literary style. To him the Revolution of 1688 stood for the highest point of constitutional development in England. He said "it has been of all Revolutions the least violent and of all Revolutions the most beneficent".

In spite of his hard work, he had taken the story down to the beginning of the reign of Queen Anne. His fifth volume appeared in 1861 posthumously. It was continued by his grand nephew Trevelyan. Even this unfinished work immediately made him take rank with Gibbon. It has been rightly said, 'Macaulay's history remains one of the most triumphant literary masterpieces of the Victorian Age'.

Contributions. His contribution to history broadly divides itself into two parts:

(1) History of England

(2) Historical Essays.

His essays are very brilliant. They are of permanent value. Some essays are very brilliant and are now read only for their style. He represented the Whig view of English history. He was the great lover of liberties. Therefore he was an unreasonable opponent of even the virtues of those whom he chose to denigrate like Charles I, Laud, Cranmer and Stratford. His praise of Cromwell redeemed the protection from an oblivion to which less seasoned historians had condemned him and therefore he paved the way for Carlyle. Among his essays many subjects are covered. Milton the poet, Frederick the despot, Pitt the Prime Minister, Warren Hastings the Pro-consul, Boswell the biographer and many others come under the sway of his inimitable pen. His contact with India persuaded him to write the two famous Indian essays Clive and Warren Hastings. Warren Hastings is the most colourful and balanced of his historical essays. Gooch rightly calls Macaulay's Warren Hastings, 'the most dazzling work of art in the author's gallery' but he adds that it was the most inaccurate of his portraits.

Macaulay's writings have been criticised by Mill and Carlyle. The chief criticism of Macaulay centres round the point that he had no regard for his sources and where he wrote sincerely his picture was vitiated by prejudice. Thompson had said, 'Greece had but one Thucydides. Rome had but one Tacitus and England had but one Macaulay'. Macaulay wrote an essay on history in which he concluded by saying that 'the ideal historian must known how to paint as well as to draw and must embrace the culture as well as the actions of mankind'.

(17) Thomas Carlyle

Thomas Carlyle (1795-1881) was the greatest moral force in the world of English Letters in the 19th century. With the solitary exception of Macaulay he combined historical scholarship with literary force to a remarkable degree.

Thomas Carlyle was born on the 4th December 1795 at Ecclefechan, Scotland. In 1814 he left the Edinburgh University without taking a degree. Then he took mathematics and met Margaret Gordon at Kirkcaly, his student. But due to the intervention of her family, his romance ended in failure. This was a great blow to Carlyle. In his teaching profession at Edinburgh he started writing. He hated poverty, snobbery, hypocricy, misery, but he also had great contempt for the masses *i.e.*, while disapproving of victimisation, he had scant regard for victim.

The German thinkers and writers greatly influenced Carlyle in his life. He started writing for the Edinburgh Encyclopaedia. In 1827 he produced the 'German Romance' in four volumes. His writings on German literature are now collected in the 'Critical Miscellaneous Essays'.

In 1826 he married Jane Welsh of Haddington. In 1833, the Carlyles left Scotland and came to London. He wrote 'French Revolution' under the banner of poverty. Accordingly to Carlyle's own admission 'the book came direct and flamingly from his heart'. This work has been described as 'one of the savagest written for several centuries, a book written by a wild man'.

From poverty he rose to prosperity in 1865 when he became Lord Rector of the Edinburgh University. At this hour of triumph he met with his worst tragedy in life. He was then informed that his wife had been dead in her carriage while driving in Hyde Park. He died in 1881 at the age of 87.

Carlyle's chief historical works were:

(1) The French Revolution,

(2) On Heroes, hero worship and the heroic deeds in history,

(3) Past and Present,

(4) Oliver Cromwell's Letters and Speeches,

(5) History of Frederick the Great — (6 Volumes),

(6) Early Kings of Norway.

No doubt the German influence on Carlyle has been overrated. Goethe exercised a tremendous influence upon Carlyle. He was the romantic historian of the 19th century in England par excellence.

The French Revolution was an immediate sensation. This book has been read for over a century and will always be in demand among those who decry inequity. It is an epic in prose flashing with the lightning and reverberating with the thunder of the stormy events. But he produced therein a thrilling story and a collection of marvellously vivid portraits. It begins with the exit of Louis XV and ends with the entry of Napoleon I into the French scene. The French Revolution became an eminent theme for study and discussion for the English speaking world with Carlyle's French Revolution.

Lady Sydney Morgan a fashionable sentimental novelist wrote: 'Faith, he says is gone out; scepticism is coming. Now faith and scepticism had nothing directly to do with the affair *i.e.*, the French Revolution. It was want and misery and oppression in the lower-class, utter corruption and incapacity in the higher that made the Road'. This was countered by a favourable review by J.S. Mill in 1837. In this review he concludes: "A most original book, original not least on its complete sincerity its disregard of the merely conventional, every idea and sentiment is given out exactly as it is thought and flesh from the soul of the writer and in such language it is most capable of representing it in the form in which it exists there".

It must be admitted that Carlyle's French Revolution suffers from important faults some arising from the circumstances of the time and others from the particularity of his philosophy. His knowledge of details was limited. He did not consult the archives; so some rediculous errors crept into his narrative. Moreover his history does not deal with the causes of the French Revolution, the economic factors and foreign solutions. Gooch says Carlyle exalted the pageants but condemned the history.

His interest and enthusiasm in Cromwell and in Frederick was the result of his philosophy of history which is that history is the biography of great men. Carlyle has been compared with Macaulay. Both were literary historians. Carlyle carried words to suit his ideas. Thus Carlyle rendered remarkable service for the historical writings.

(18) G.M. Trevelyan

George Macaulay Trevelyan (1876-1962) was the third son of Sir George Otto Trevelyan, the nephew of Lord Macaulay. He was educated at Harrow and at Trinity College, Cambridge and developed a taste for history and dislike for 'dry biscuit' mathematics.

Lord Acton exercised a tremendous influence upon Trevelyan. Moreover Gibbon's influence over Trevelyan was so great in his writings. His main works were:

(1) England under the Stuarts,
(2) Garibaldi's defence of Roman Republic,
(3) History of England,
(4) English Social History — A Survey of six centuries.

His Social History of England is one of the most famous works. Speaking of his History of England he himself said, "some say very soon perhaps it will be replaced by any other work and it will serve many generations to come.

After the death of J.B. Bury in 1927, the Regius Professorship of Modern History at Cambridge was offered to Trevelyan by Stanley Baldwin. During his Professorship he wrote the three volumes of 'England under Queen Anne' which he himself declared was 'my best work except perhaps the Garibaldis'.

Trevelyan's 'Clio, a Muse and other Essays' is a collection of beautiful essays on various subjects some of which the 'Clio the Muser and the Present Position of History' are historical.

It goes without saying that Trevelyan treated history as an art. According to Henry R. Winkler, "George Macauley Trevelyan, a recent student of historiography has written, has done more than any other living writer to restore history to its earlier station as a literary art which instructs and entertains the general public and professionals alike".

In the field of social history G.M. Trevelyan made a wonderful contribution. His famous definition of social history is that "social history is History minus political history". Though his definition has been attacked by many comers, yet the fact cannot be denied that his work possesses great educative value and neo-sociological techniques. According to J.R. Hale "Trevelyan was a great writer, a wise and generous and scrupulously fair man. He will remain a great name in the history of English historiography for his personality, his craftsman-ship and his success, but probably no famous historian has made a smaller contribution to the inner history of his subject.

Thus G.M. Trevelyan contributed much to historiography and paved the way for future historians.

(19) Arnold J. Toynbee

Arnold Joseph Toynbee (1889-1975) was born in London on 14th April 1889. He was educated at Winchester and Balliol, Oxford. He taught at Oxford and London. Later he worked for the British government in the foreign office as a diplomat and at the universities as a professional historian. As a teacher he started with Greek literature and history and soon made an extensive study of the civilisations of ancient, medieval and modern times. According to Dr. N. Subramanian "The Far-East and India are the Achilles' heel of his massive scholarship". For sometime he worked as the Director of Studies in the Royal Institute of International Affairs and Research Professor of International history at London.

Toynbee's major works include 'Nationality and War', 'Greek Historical Thought', 'Civilisation on Trial', 'Experiences' and 'A Historian's View of Religion'. But his magnum opus is the 'Study of History' in twelve volumes. The Cambridge History of English Literature praises it as "the greatest single handed historical achievement since "The Decline and Fall". In this immense work he studies not the fortunes of an empire, a people or a country, but he is concerned with all the great civilisations he has listed for his purposes of study. Toynbee's 'Study of History' "is the most ambitious project in historical synthesis ever attempted by a single author". For the learning and erudition capacity for comprehension, for classification and interpretation his work is unrivalled.

It is very clear that Toynbee's interesting personality is totally reflected in his 'Study of History'. It is considered his major contribution to historical theory. His work has two aspects: (1) a massive collection of historical data and (2) the meaning assigned to it. While his scholarship has been readily accepted, the meaning assigned by him to history has been severely criticised by critics. Toynbee advises that a historian should not study the history of a nation or a country but that of a Civilisation. He believes that the growth and decline of a Civilisation can be easily understood in terms of twin principles of 'challenge and response'. Toynbee refuted the plea that there is a law of fate which governs human societies, although he never forgets to stress importance to God in history. He believes that human beings are helped by God who sets a divine plan. Within the limits of this plan, the man has freedom and will and can successfully defy the challenge in many ways. Thus Toynbee's conception of history got beyond the range of secular history.

There are certain similarities between Toynbee and Spengler. Spengler was interested in making a study over different cultures whereas Toynbee speaks of civilisations.

Spengler refers to cultures and Toynbee studies all civilisations.

In this connection Toynbee is not pessimistic about Western Civilisation as Spengler.

Many criticisms have been levelled against the views of Toynbee. They are as follows:

(1) It is pointed out that Toynbee was a determinist He collects a vast array of historical data in order to reach a forgone conclusion. But Toynbee stoutly repudiated the allegation that he was a determinist. "He said he was not one. But he also said that the fate of human civilisations will be 'determined' by the manner of response to the challenge that is posed". He pointed out that the response is not predetermined. It was the result of free will of man and can defy challenge in a variety of ways.

(2) The famous Dutch historian Pieter Geyl criticised Toynbee in the following manner: Toynbee bases his argument on 20 cases selected at random from the histories of all the peoples of all the centuries. He blamed that Toynbee selected the 20 cases according to his convenience. But the 20 cases are selected cases, selected out of 200 or 200,000. Even if they (the very same 20 cases) had been presented in a different way the results would have been different from that of Toynbee's conclusions.

(3) It has been said that Toynbee was not quite correct in presuming that there is only a single pattern of history. But Pieter Geyl while answering to Toynbee said that one of the greatest things to realise about history is its infinite complexity and the historical phenomenon and incidents keep on changing that the effort to reduce them to fixed relationship can never lead to anything but disappointment.

(4) A.J. Toynbee's 'study of History' has been ridiculed by M.E. Barnes.

(5) A.L. Rowse criticises Toynbee in the following words: "Toynbee imposes 'his' patterns upon the subject seeks to be a Prophet and provide answers to the contemporary problems that distract us, and he adds rather insultingly to the gallery, especially American — hence his uncritical popular success, especially in America. But this object is neither the province nor the function of history. It is indeed contrary to its nature — to impose a thesis upon the facts accurately, patiently without prejudice. Thesis — history is false history".

(6) According to D.H. Fischer, "Toynbee's work suffers from the holiest fallacy that all metaphysical historians by definition are guilty of this mistake".

(7) Walsh reminds us that in dealing with the life cycles of civilisations Toynbee resembles Vico and Herder. Toynbee calls the stages in the development of a civilisation, birth (genesis), growth, breakdown, dissolution and death.

To him all history is the fulfilment of some divine plan. Within the bounds of this plan, however, man is allowed freedom of will, freedom of choice. The individual therefore is the direct creator of history *i.e.*, ... the direct creator of civilisation; he says that 'man cannot live outside society although history is made by the individual and not by society'.

In spite of all the criticisms mentioned above the very fact that he is the most discussed among historians today shows that his influence is enormous. He came to be regarded as the universal historian.

17

Chinese Historical Writing

From the earliest times, the Chinese have shown a marked inclination to historical writing. The nature of historical works also represent wide-ranging interests. Many works have been written by the Chinese on different aspects of government machinery, monasteries etc.

K.S. Latourette in his book "The Chinese, their history and culture" compares the Chinese with the Hindus and says 'in a marked contrast with the peoples of India the Chinese have been historically minded'.

Li-chi, The Book of Rites: In this book, the historians' views of the past are expressed in the most exalted terms. It contains many essays. This work was compiled during the Han dynasty (202 B.C -220 A.D). The ideal of a social order wherein people lived in 'Grand Unity' is described in many lucid passages. In this connection the early conception of history revealing social order with noble elements deserves to be noted.

During the Han Dynasty cyclical pattern was accepted by the Chinese historians. It means the cyclical sequence of events discussed by those historians were explained in this book. This cyclical pattern repeated itself through several centuries. This was the view of ancient Chinese historians.

Ssu-ma-Chien: In the reign of Wu-ti, Ssu-ma-Chien the greatest among the Chinese historians wrote his great history called the 'Shih-Chi' which means 'historical records'.

Ssu-ma-Chien was born in 145 B.C. His father was a court astrologer. When Chien was very young, he memorised the text of antiquity and he used these as his source material. He travelled extensively. He may be called the Father of History in Oriental Lands.

After the death of his father Chien became the court astrologer. He brought about the reform of the Calendar.

The Shih-Chi covers the history of China from the beginning of Ssu-ma-Chien's own day. It includes not only significant political events but gives the biographies of important persons; chronological tables of battles, economic data, the calendar and so forth. It goes without saying that work was a model for later dynastic histories. It was written at the close of the 2nd and the beginning of the first century B.C.

The Tso-Chuan

It is another kind of history. It is in the form of a chronicle and events are listed year by year. The most reputed among such chronicle was the 'Tyu-Chih-tung-chien? by Ssu-ma-Kuang (1019 - 1086). This chronicle covered the history of Chinese development from late in the Chou to beginning of the Sung periods. This work illustrates the historical mindedness of the Sung dynasty in a remarkable way. It covered the period from the 5th century B.C. to the close of the five dynasties.

Ssu-ma-Kuang was a politician. He wrote his history when he was in power.

Tung-Chien-Chishipenna

Yuan-Chu prepared a history called 'Tung-Chien-Chishipenna' which means 'root causes and effects of affairs recorded in the universal mirror'. Generally the Chinese were concerned with the causes and effects of historical phenomena. This is seen from the above work. Moreover the Chinese believed in the chain of causation.

There are many special histories on different aspects of Chinese life. The Chinese have produced a large volume of local histories and gazetteers. They are very descriptive in nature. They are statistical geography of China.

In China there are 5000 gazetteers. We get a lot of information about the governmental machinery also. We also get some informations about the civil services of China,

China has a large volume of inscriptions. These have been compiled and studied. Treatises have been written on them by the Chinese themselves.

No doubt they introduced historical criticism in their art of historiography. It is really an important innovation of the Chinese. They have also produced encyclopaedia and anthologies which contains a large fund of historical material.

The modern historical tradition of China is influenced by communist ideology. Economic analysis, conditions of the peasants, toilers and workers, the living conditions of the masses, have all been assiduously unearthed under the new inspiration. In this way the Chinese have done a wonderful thing in the study of historiography.

18
Arab Historical Writing

During the medieval period the European historiography was in the hands of Christian theologians whereas the Muslims in the Middle East were creating their own traditions of historical writing which was theological in some respects and scientific in many others. Serious historical chronicling started only after the founding of Islam by the Prophet.

The Muslims started a historiographical tradition from the Islamic point of view. The early Caliphs engaged chroniclers to record their early ancestry. They also engaged court historians for the same purpose. The anecdotes connected with the Prophet became a chief source of early Islamic history for Muslims of later generations.

After founding of the Abbasid Caliphate in 750 A.D. serious historiographical efforts were made in the Middle East by the Muslims. This took the shape of biographies, anecdotes and episodic history, genealogies as well as collection of tradition. The earliest of biography was that of the Prophet's life written by Ibn Ishaq. Ibn Hisham also wrote a biography of Mohammad in 834 A.D.

The Muslims system of chronology was very accurate since they followed the Hejira era. Al Firdausi (935-1020 A.D.) wrote in Persian 'The Book of Kings' and this served as a model for the Arabian historians.

'The history of the wars of the Prophet' was written by Al-Wequidi. He was a great historian of the Abbasid period.

Al Baladhuri of the 9th century wrote the early achievements of the Muslims in his 'Conquest of the Countries'. This is an authoritative work on the expansion of Islam.

During this period, Dinawari composed the 'History of Arabia and Persia'.

Ibin Abi Tahir wrote his 'The History of Baghdad and its Caliphs' in a fascinating style. This is a standard work on the Caliphate of Baghdad.

Al Tahori (838-923) was a towering historian among the early Muslims. He travelled widely. His monumental work was 'The Annals of the Apostles and Kings'. He brought it down to A.D. 915. He collected enormous materials. Those materials were used by most of the later historians.

Al Masudi was a great historian. He lived during the first half of the 10th century. He was an encyclopaedist. His 'Meadows of Gold' contain social historical material. He has been called the Herodotus of the Arabs. But this analogy is not true since the Father of History was more truly a historian.

In 970 Ibn Miskawaihi wrote the 'Experience of the Nations' which is noted for its impartiality. According to a critic, "In the work of Miskawaihi Arabic historical composition seems to reach its highest point".

Baha-al-Din (1185-1234) wrote a good biography of 'Saladin'. It gives a graphic picture of Saladin and his achievements.

Al-Binmi (973-1048) lived in the court of Mahmud of Ghazni. He stayed in India for sometime. He studied her culture there. He was an able sociologist and astronomer. He was the author of the 'Kitab-ul-Hind' (1030). In it he expressed his admirations for the cultural achievements of the Hindus. It is unique in Muslim literature.

Ibn Khaldun (1332-1406) has been called the first modern historian by many scholars. He was the ablest Arab historian. He could reflect on the purpose of history. H.E. Barnes calls him the Roger Bacon of medieval historiography. He believed that history must relate not only to political developments but must be concerned with social problems also.

In the 'Prolegomena to Universal History' he sets forth his views on history very beautifully. According to him history was the science of the origin and development of society and civilisation.

Ibn Khaldun wrote his "Universal history" in seven volumes. He stressed the need to include various social aspects under the purview of historical writing.

Flint calls him the founder of the "science of history" and this tribute is fully justified in the context of the historians stress on source material and its veracity.

S.N. Fisher states : "Since he considered the factors of climate, geography, economics and culture, Ibn Khaldun can be called the first modern historian".

Abu Zaid (1332-1406), a Tunisian—who was a contemporary of Timur, wrote his own biography. His writings throw light on contemporary political developments. He may be credited with the theory of growth and decay of social groups.

19

Historians of India

(A) ANCIENT

(i) Banar, (ii) Bilhanar & (iii) Kalhanar

In the ancient period our people had failed to write their history. They did not show any interest in writing their history. But during the medieval and modern periods of their history historiography has made notable progress. It was generally opined that the Indians totally lacked the historical sense. But this view is discredited by the few historical texts, local chronicles like those of Nepal, Kashmir, Gujarat and other places.

In his "History of the Tamils" P.T. Srinivasa Iyengar observes "If chronology is the eye of history ancient Indian history will have always to be blind".

K.A. Nilakanda Sastri says, "Literature in other countries, the bedrock of history in India it is often a snare".

Even though we are left without historical literature, we have abundant historical material in lithic inscriptions, copper plates, coins etc., which help us partially at least to reconstruct our history.

The Hindu Princes of ancient India maintained in their courts Sutas and Magadhas whose business was perhaps to maintain a sort of official records; but their exact functions are not quite clear though possibly they were some sort of genealogists.

It is said that the ancient Indians had a sense of history but left no historical writing. Later on it began to develop in India. Now it is better to see some of the historians of India and their historical writings in this connection.

(i) Banar: Bana Bhatta was the court poet of Harsha. His period was from 590 to 647 A.D. He was a Brahmin by birth. He belonged to the Vatsyayana family. He was a native of Pritivikuta on the banks of the Sone. The boy who was orphaned early in his life sought service in the court of Harsha, the ruler of Kanauj.

Bana was a man of letters. He wrote his book in Sanskrit. He is more famous as the author of the 'Kadambari' a romance written in a style admired by Indian critics.

Bana's 'Harsha Charita' is a historical work in the sense it deals with the life and doings of Harsha, a historical figure.

His 'Harsha Charita' is in eight chapters and does not tell us all about the hero. S.K. De. says, "The sum total of the story is no more than an incident in Harsha's career — it cannot be said that the picture either is full or satisfactory from the historical point of view".

Dr. A.B. Keith says, "What Bana supplies to history is the vivid picture of the army of the life of the court and the avocations of Brahmins and their friends".

In short the work may be classified as a historical novel dealing with high political matters by a contemporary. But it cannot be denied that he is guilty of exaggerations and flattery and of omissions like the failure to mention Rajyavardhana's accession to the throne of Thaneshwar. In spite of all this, it is considered as a great historical treasure for Harsha's history.

(ii) Bilhanar: Bilhana was a Kashmiri. He wrote his ' Vikramangadeva Charita' before 1088 A.D. He was patronised by Someswara I, father of Vikramaditya VI (1076-1126), Chalukya king of Kalyani.

This Vikramaditya was the hero of the Charita. The patron conferred on the poet the title Vidyapati. His play Kamasundari is a comedy dealing with the marriage of Kamadeva I of Anhilwad with Mayamalladeva. But his fame as a romantic biographer in verse rests on the former work.

Bilhana's work is helpful to us to verify certain historical facts we get from other sources regarding the career and achievements of Vikramaditya VI.

The 'Charita' mentions a few historical facts like the battles fought by Vikramaditya VI against his brother Someswara II. The historical value of this work is not much, though the author by Indian standards was possibly a good poet.

(iii) Kalhana: In ancient times, the inhabitants of Kashmir developed a strong historical tradition. Kashmir was well known as a seat of Sanskrit learning. According to R.C. Majumdar, "There is only one historical work, properly so called written by Kalhana in the 12th century. This is "Rajatarangini" which deals with the history of Kashmir from the earliest times upto the date of the composition of that work".

Kalhana was the author of 'Rajatarangini'. He was the son of Kanpaga a Minister of King Harsha of Kashmir, After the death of Harsha, he did not take up any new assignment under the new rulers, but his position gave an opportunity to the young Kalhana to develop an interest in history.

Kalhana studied the different chronicles on Kashmir and the local puranas but he was neither pleased nor satisfied by their versions. He wanted to bring out a true and reliable historical work on his state.

Kalhana started his monumental work in 1148 A.D. and completed it within two years. Rajatarangini (chronicles of Kashmir) is only a general history of Kashmir and did not attach significance to any particular dynasty. While writing the work, Kalhana made extensive use of the past resources, contemporary documents, edicts, inscriptions, coins, ancient monuments etc.

Kalhana also consulted the eleven earlier chronicles, the Nilamata Purana, the works of Sourata, Kshmendra's chronicles on Kashmir, Coins, decrees and verbal traditions. All these clearly indicate that Kalhana was able to understand the fundamental principles of historiography.

According to K.A.N. Sastri, "Kalhana laid down some correct principles of historical writing for himself though he was not able to observe them always owing to the defects in the sources accessible to him".

In the opinion of an eminent historian, "Kalhana's notion of historiography is a clear improvement on that of romantic chronicles like Bana and Bilhana."

Rajatarangini is a work of approximately 8,000 highly polished verses. It is divided into three major divisions. Book I to III narrate the past events in the light of the prevailing conditions. Book IV to VI refer to the histories of Karkota and Utpalaysa dynasties. Book VII and VIII provide information on the two dynasties which ruled in Kashmir.

The scholarly work Rajatarangini has been translated and edited in several languages. The most popular in that is in English by Aruel Stein.

Kalhana was of the view that Vidhata the Creator and God of Gods, influences the course of history. He held the view that king Mihiregula was a tyrant, yet he was protected by the gods. Some of his conceptions about government were useful and sound in principles. He insisted that king should be strong and rigid, but at the same time he should be benevolent and considerate.

Kalhana too had certain shortcomings. He frequently accepted legend and stories as true and reliable accounts, often he was led by blind faith and superstitious ideas. In spite of all these defects, Kalhana was an honest historian and his Rajatarangini was a sincere attempt at providing a true history in Sanskrit verse.

Thus Kalhana rendered remarkable service to historiography.

(B) MEDIEVAL

(a) Amir Khusrau (1252-1325): Amir Khusrau was a poet. He wrote some books which give us a peep into the political and social history of his times. He was born in Uttar Pradesh. He was a Turk. He had seen the reigns of Sultans Balban to Ghiyasud-din Tughlak. He was patronised by Kaikubad, Jalalud-din Khilji, Alaud-din Khilji, Mubarak Shah and Ghiyasud-din Khilji.

Amir Khusrau was a prolific writer. His historical work 'Miftah-ul-Futulf deals with the victories of Jalalud-din Khilji.

The 'Tughlaq Nama' deals with the events of early days of Ghiyasud-din Tughlak's reign and the Tarikhi-Alai was the victories of Alaud-din Khilji's Deccan campaigns.

Amir Khusrau witnessed some of the events in person during the Deccan Campaigns. His capacity for innocent flattery in exquisite Persian was retained for him the conveted position of five Sultans.

(b) Alberuni: Muhammad Abu Ahmad Alberuni also known as Abu Raihan was born in Khiva in Central Asia in 973 A.D. After distinguishing himself in science and literature, he became a councillor of the ruler of Khiva. When Muhamad Ghazni invaded Khawarizm, Alberuni was taken prisoner of war along with others to Ghazni. Later when Muhamad of Ghazni invaded India Alberuni accompanied him to India.

Alberuni visited India many times and utilised his stay in India to learn about the country. He conversed with the Pandits and learnt about their religion, science and culture.

Alberuni's mastery of Hindu and Greek astrology turned him to become the court astrologer of Sultan Masud, son of Sultan Muhamad. Later he devoted his time to studies and wrote Tahkik-i-Hind'. It was perhaps the most important one.

In his book entitled Tahkik-i-Hind (Reality of Hindustan) Alberuni gives an account of the religious, literary and scientific traditions of India. The book is divided into 80 chapters and one is able to get information on all aspects of life. He praised the Hindus for their good knowledge in philosophy, mathematics and astronomy.

Alberuni gives a detailed account of the customs of Hindus in his book. He was greatly impressed by the literary works of the Hindus. He refers to the four Vedas, eighteen Puranas, twenty Smriti books as well as Mahabharata. He tells that Hindus believed in one eternal God. He mentions about the idol-worship of the Hindus.

Alberuni gives a graphic picture of the political conditions of India during his life time. He also refers to the economic conditions prevailing in that time. Thus the account provided by Albemni is quite graphic and charming. According to B.N. Luniya, "The work of Albemni is unique in Muslim literature......"

(c) Barani (1286-1359): Maulana Ziyauddin Barani was born in 1286 in a Saiyyad family of Kaithal. That family members held high positions in the administration of the Khiljis. Barani too occupied an important position under the Khiljis.

Later Barani became the courtier of Muhammad Bin Tughluq. Tughluq appreciated his wide knowledge of history and scholarship and showered favours on him. He died in the year 1359 A.D. at the age of 73 in poverty.

Barani showed keen interest in history. In his 'Tarikh-i-Firozshahi' he showed the qualities of a good historian. He believed that truthfulness, impartiality, honesty and fearlessness are the essential qualities of a true historian. With all those admirable qualities, he could not rise up to the level of a great historian. Orthodoxy and fanaticism blunted the vision of his thinking.

Barani wrote ten historical books. But some of them are yet to be traced. Among the ten works, the two well known are:

(1) Tarikh-i-Firozshahi and (2) Fatawa-i-Jahandari

According to B.N. Luniya "Barani begins his work (Tarikh-i-Firozshahi) with the long discussion on historiography and the use of historical studies". He had elaborately covered the periods of Balban and Alaud-din Khilji. He has described the virtues and vices of Muhammad Bin Tughluq. To quote Barani "The Sultan wantonly shed the blood of innocent Muslims so much so that a stream of blood was always seen flowing before the threshold of the palace".

Barani's next important work is Fatawa-i-Jahandari. "It is a kind of ideal political code, which he would like a Muslim king to follow". The work describes certain principles of administration and significant ideals of government. He divided the work into two major divisions: (1) Principles and ideals of administration and (2) Examples from history to illustrate them.

No doubt Barani's style of writing is very fine. His style of writing has been widely praised by the historical writers. He followed a simple, clear and lucid style. He avoided the highly ornamental style which was then in fashion. "He possessed a facile pen and writes in a clear and unostentatious way".

Barani had certain defects also. His likes and dislikes are revealed in his writings. The chronological order of events in his narration is defective. His sunni predilections were quite strong. He was also anti-Hindu to a great extent. He had strong religious bias and so he judged people of other denominations harshly; his contemporaneity with the events and men he was describing made it difficult for him to write objectively. With all these handicaps Barani wrote admirable histories. Thus he did a lot to historical writings.

(d) Abul Fazl: The most illustrious name among the historians of the Mughal period was Abul Fazl. His monumental works were 'Akbamama' and the 'Aini Akbari'. They are very important sources for history of the reign of Akbar.

Abul Fazl was born in 1551 as the son of Shaik Mubarak of Nagaur. He was attached to Akbar's court.

Abul Fazl started his career as a teacher. Later on he became his favourite in the court.

Abul Fazl's 'Akbarnama' is a detailed account of Akbar's reign. At the orders of Akbar, he wrote the work. It took seven years for him to complete the monumental work and he submitted to the Mughal emperor, Akbar. While writing the book, Abul Fazl states "I spent much labour and research in collecting the records and narratives of the Majesty's action, and I was for long time interrogating the servants of the state and the old members of the illustrious family. I examined both prudent, truth speaking old men and active minded, right actioned young men and reduced their statements to writing. The royal commands were issued to the provinces that those who from old service remembered with certainty or with admixture of doubt the events of the past, should copy out their notes and memoranda and transmit them to court".

Abul Fazl's analytical mind and intellectual gift greatly helped him to write the work. He possessed a high style in Persian language and strove hard in finding out the truth. The chronology is generally accurate; his statements are sober and remarks even towards his enemies are dispassionate. So he came to be regarded as more a literary, artist than a scientific historian.

V.A. Smith criticises him as an unblushing flatterer of Akbar.

Aini Akbari gives a detailed account of the revenue system, administrative regulations and statistical data.

In addition to these works Abul Fazl translated the 'Gita' also. Many of his private letters are collected into the 'Ruqqati-Abul Fazl'.

(C) MODERN PERIOD

(i) James Tod (1782-1835): James Tod was born in Islington. His father had settled in the Uttar Pradesh as a planter. His uncles were in the East India Company. James Tod himself entered the company's military service. By 1800 he became a lieutenant. In 1805 he was assigned to the service of English Agent at Sindhia's court. In 1818 he became political agent to the Western Rajput states and was in that position till he retired in 1822.

James Tod collected a large quantity of historical materials on central India and Rajasthan during the years from 1812 to 1817. When he was in

Rajasthan he developed a close friendship with many Rajput chiefs and equipped himself for the masterly work on Rajasthan which was to make him immortal.

In 1824 he became a Major; in 1826 a Lieutenant-Colonel. In 1835 he passed away while doing business in London Bank.

James Tod's contribution to history consists of the annals and antiquities of Rajasthan and the travels in Western India. The latter was published posthumously. The former were published between 1829 and 1832 in two volumes.

"The Annals and Antiquities of Rajasthan" immediately became a classic. It is one of the most sympathetic accounts of India written by a foreigner. It deals with the history and sociology of the Rajputs.

James Tod was attracted by the glittering glamour of Rajput feudalism and the romantic veneer which covered the surface of their feudal life. He gave a realistic and true picture of the Rajasthan he knew and a romantic picture of the Rajputana he imagined.

James Tod represented the contemporary romantic historiography in India and his work was a combination of a lot of gazeteer information written with the romantic pen of Sir Walter Scott. There are some errors in regard to chronology and even geography. In short he has given a graphic account of the Rajputs in his great work. Dr. Qanungo says "in Tod the Hellas of Hindustan found a Herodotus".

(ii) Sir Alexander Cunningham (1814-1893): Sir Alexander Cunningham was a pioneer in Indian historical research and in archaeology.

Sir Alexander Cunningham was educated at Christ Church, Oxford. He came to India in 1833. He began his career as a military engineer in the Sikh wars. He became the Director of Archaeology in 1862. He worked very hard to bring forth ancient historical antiquities. He published the annual reports of his work between 1862-1884.

Sir Alexander Cunningham did a wonderful work in archaeology. So he is truly considered the Father of Indian Archaeology.

All his efforts are embodied in the 23 volumes containing the results of his survey of the central and northern parts of India.

Sir Alexander Cunningham edited the 'Corpus Inscriptionum Indecorum I' *i.e.*, Asoka's Inscriptions.

He was the author of the 'Ancient Geography of India', 'The Stupa of Barhut', "The book of Indian eras" etc. Thus he laid the foundation for the collection of non-literary sources. From this we come to understand the interest evinced by the British scholars for historiography.

(iii) Vincent Smith (1843-1920): Vincent Arthur Smith was the last great English historian of India of the old school. Inspite of his innumerable works, he found time to write history. He became one of the great historians of India. Historiography since the days of Orme had passed through many vicissitudes.

V.A. Smith wrote his 'Early History of India (1904) from 600 B.C. to the Muslim conquest with special reference to Alexander's campaigns in India.

V.A. Smith's 'Oxford History of India' made him at once famous as the first really complete history of India.

Smith was fifth of thirteen children of his father. He had a brilliant career in his college. In 1871 he joined in the Indian Civil Service. He held a number of important administrative posts in that service.

Smith married Mary Elizabeth and became the father of three sons and a daughter. He retired from service in 1900. He lived for 20 years after retirement. During this period he spent his time on Indian historical studies. He became a C.I.E. and a member of the Royal Asiatic Society.

V.A. Smith's major works are:

(1) Asoka, the Buddhist Emperor of India.

(2) Akbar, the Great Mughal.

(3) A History of Fine Art in India and Ceylon.

(4) Catalogue of Coins in Indian Museum.

(5) Oxford History of India.

His 'Asoka' in spite of many subsequent publications on that subject remains a masterpiece.

Besides, his Catalogue of the Coins is a unique work on numismatics.

His Oxford History of India published in 1918 was the first full history of India written with an accuracy and in a style not known before. His British period has been much criticised. In spite of that he is considered as a great British historian of India.

(iv) Henry Heras (1800-1955): Rev. Henry Heras came to India in 1922 when he was thirty two years old. He was appointed to the prestigious post of Professor of Indian History at St. Xavier's College.

Father Heras spent more than three decades in this country studying and expounding the history of this land. He was quite versatile and spoke as eloquently as he wrote. He wrote on the 'Pallavas' and 'Vijayanagar'. But his magnum opus however was his work on the 'Indus Valley Civilisation'. Father Heras was famed as an eloquent speaker, impressive teacher and original thinker.

Father Heras pioneered the view that the Indus seals bear a script the language of which was proto-Tamil a controversy which has been gaining momentum since then. Thus for historical writing, Father Heras has done a lot.

(v) G.S. Sardesai (1865-1959): G.S. Sardesai belonged to the family of Mavlankars. Sardesai means a hereditary office held in Maharashtra.

Sardesai left the secondary school when he was very young. Then he married to Gangu Bai. His collegiate education was taken care of by his father-in-law.

Sardesai graduated in 1888, and from 1889 to 1925 he served the Baroda State by taking up an assignment in the Gaekwad palace. He was personal clerk to the ruler and so he had abundant travel facilities.

Seeing the talent of Sardesai the Gaekwad asked him to translate Machiavelli's 'Prince' and Seeley's 'Expansion of England' into Mahratti. His greatest contribution to the history of the Mahrattas is known as Mahratti Riyasat. These presented the history of the Mahrattas from beginning to 1848 in eight volumes.

Sardesai's style is remarkably lucid. He was a great friend of J.N. Sarkar. It was Sarkar who persuaded Sardesai to write in English. His 'Shivaji and his Times' is considered as a great work. No doubt he is considered as the greatest Mahratta historian.

'Sarkar and Sardesai combination gave 62 volumes of original documents to the students of Mahratta history'. Finally Sardesai wrote the one book which every student of Mahratta history reads, 'The New History of the Mahrattas' in English. At the age of 80 true wisdom in regard to historical writing dawned upon him and he wrote very correctly. ".......I will now allow documents to speak rather than impose my views upon the readers."

(vi) J.N. Sarkar (1870-1958): Sir Jadunath Sarkar's contributions to historical writings cannot be under estimated or minimised. His name is inseparable from that of Sardesai. What Sardesai had been to the Mahratta, Sarkar had been to the Mughals.

According to G.P. Gooch "he has been the greatest Indian historian and he remains the master of us all."

J.N. Sarkar was born in 1870 in an eastern district of Bengal now in Bangladesh. He had a distinguished academic career and took his M.A. in English literature in 1892 standing university first.

J.N. Sarkar started his career as an English lecturer. In 1901 he published his first research paper. It was on 'India of Aurangzeb.' Thereafter he switched his loyalty from English literature over to History. He was promoted to the Indian Educational Service in 1918. He retired from services in 1926. Just before retirement he was nominated Vice Chancellor of Calcutta University.

J.N. Sarkar was honoured by the Royal Asiatic Society of Britain in 1923.

In 1929 he was knighted by the British Government. The Government had conferred also the C.I.E. on him in 1926.

'The royal historical society of England which at no time has more than 30 honorary members in the whole world included Sarkar in its membership. The American historical society appointed him as honorary life member and in all Asia he was the only scholar to have been so honoured.

J.N. Sarkar was well versed in English, Sanskrit, Persian and Mahratti in addition he learned Hindi, French, German, Portuguese and Rajasthani, Bengali was his mother tongue.

J.N. Sarkar's masterpiece was the 'History of Aurangzeb' in five volumes. He spent 25 years to write this masterpiece. In addition to this he prepared also a 'Shorter History of Aurangzeb' in one volume. Simultaneously he was working on 'Shivaji and his Times'. His last work was 'Military History of India', posthumously published.

J.N. Sarkar devoted most of his time to write on Mughals. In other words mostly he wrote on the Mughals and particularly Aurangzeb, Mughal administration, fall of the Mughal empire. Aurangzeb and Shivaji were his favourite subjects.

Thus J.N. Sarkar contributed much to Indian historical writings.

(vii) K.A.N. Sastri: K.A.N. Sastri was born on August 12, 1892 in Tirunelveli District, Tamilnadu. He had a brilliant educational career. He graduated from the Madras University with a first class first in his M.A. Degree Examination. For sometime he served as Professor of history in Tirunelveli and then in Benaras. He was the Principal of Sri Meenakshi College, Chidambaram during 1920-29 and then it became the illustrious Annamalai University that it is now.

In 1929 K.A.N. Sastri became Professor of Indian history and Archaeology at the University of Madras. He held that position till his retirement in 1946. A few years later he took up the Professorship of Indology in the Mysore University. Then the UNESCO provided funds for an Institute of Traditional Cultures in Madras. He was nominated Director of this Institute and he held that unique position till 1972.

K.A.N. Sastri was a pioneer in the field of dynastic studies in South Indian history. He was a learned Sanskrit Scholar. He is as good at archaeology as in history and a distinguishing feature of Sastri's contribution is that whatever he writes is always readable and useful to future historians. He produced quite a number of standard works. They are:

(1) The Pandyan Kingdom,
(2) The History of the Cholas,
(3) The History of South India,
(4) Foreign Notices of South India,
(5) Sources of Indian History,
(6) The Sangam Age — its cults and cultures,
(7) Historical Method in Relation to Indian History,
(8) The Development of Religion in South India,
(9) Studies in the History of Srivijaya,
(10) Comprehensive History of India.

K.A.N. Sastri's — "The Pandyan Kingdom" was among the first books to portray dynastic history. His 'Cholas' undoubtedly gives him the first rank among Indian historians. According to Dr. N. Subramanian,' "Prof. Sastri writes in a forthright fashion and is intolerant of scant and history written to please the gallery."

(viii) S. Krishnaswamy Iyengar (1871-1953): S. Krishnaswamy was born at Sakkottai near Kumbakonam. When he was eleven years old, he lost his father. He was educated at Bangalore. He did well at school. He was deeply interested in Physics and Mathematics. But he turned from Mathematics to History. Soon after taking his M.A. in history he published a dissertation on the "History of Mysore under the Udayars".

S.K. Iyengar had intimate contact with reputed epigraphists like Hultzeh and V. Venkaiah. As early as 1901 he started his work on Chola history.

S.K. Iyengar had developed taste in Sanskrit and in Tamil and from very early days cultivated the practice of writing learned historical articles in Tamil many of which appeared in the Sentamil.

Before he took to teaching history he was teaching English at the Central College, Bangalore.

In 1914 he occupied the chair of Indian History and Archaeology in the University of Madras. Moreover he was the first occupant of that exalted chair. The illustrious school of Madras started its brilliant career with Iyengar, its rising sun.

S.K. Iyengar published his "South India and her Mohammadan Invaders" in 1921.

In 1918 he wrote "The Beginnings of South Indian History." S.K. Iyengar's other works are:

(1) Contributions of South India to Indian Culture.
(2) Manimekalai in its historical setting.

(3) Evolution of Hindu Administrative Institutions in South India.

(4) The History of Tirupati.

(5) Sources of Vijayanagar History.

S.K. Iyengar edited Sewell's "Historical Inscriptions of South India." His "Sources of Vijayanagar History" prepared the ground for the more comprehensive "Further sources" by Sastri and Venkataramanayya.

S.K. Iyengar was deeply interested in Sangam history. He wrote his chapters on South Indian History in volume III of the Cambridge History of India. For sometime he was the editor of the journal of Indian History.

S.K. Iyengar retired from the University of Madras on 1st November 1929.

Along with V. Kanagasabhai and P. Sundaram Pillai, he was a pioneer in Tamil historical studies. The encouragement he gave to historical studies in Madras was immense and the credit for founding a respectable school of history there belongs to him, though the responsibility for bringing it to its present position belongs to others. Thus S.K. Iyengar contributed much to historical writings.

(ix) K.M. Panickar: Sardar K.M. Panickar was born at Kovalam in Kerala in 1895.

K.M. Panickar was educated in the Madras Christian College and in Christ Church, Oxford, passed out with a First Class and after qualifying for the bar returned to India.

K.M. Panickar started his teaching career in Aligarh Muslim University. He continued in that teaching profession till 1922. After that he had served in a variety of capacities as publisher, state government servant, editor, diplomat and finally Vice Chancellor.

K.M. Panickar had earned a very good name and fame for his historical writings. He had natural flair for history. He wrote extremely well, but spoke moderately well.

While he was in England he published in 1918 Indian Nationalism, its principles and its history. He was endowed with a natural gift of original analysis of historical problems and in presenting them in English as well as in Malayalam.

In 1921 he wrote "Nur Jehan" and "Kurukshetra Title Kandari", the former a play and the latter a poem in Malayalam.

In 1922 he became editor of the Swarajyam Madras. In 1924 he founded and started editing the Hindustan Times in Delhi. In 1925 he resigned the editorship.

In 1925-27 he published his masterpiece 'The Native States in India." Later in 1928 he published "The British Crown and the Indian States."

In 1933 he was appointed minister for foreign affairs in Patiala and became secretary to the chamber of Princes.

In 1947 his well known "Survey of Indian History" was published.

In 1948 he was appointed ambassador to China where he delivered lectures which were collected and published as the "Background of India".

In 1959 he presented his magnum opus "Asia and Western Dominance." For some time he served as ambassador to Egypt and Sweden. His other works are:

(1) In Two Chinas.

(2) Geographical factors in Indian History.

(3) Hindu Society at cross-roads.

(4) The Afro-Asian States and their Problems.

(5) Commonsense about India.

In the fag end of his life he was Vice-Chancellor of the University of Kashmir and later of Mysore where he died on 11th December 1963. Sardar was the title conferred on him by the Maharaja of Bikaner.

From the works of Panickar we come to understand his deep sense of materialism which was inherent in him had interfered with his attitude of objectivity and balanced judgement. In short there is no denying the vast scholarship, close observation intelligent expression and genuine sympathies of Sardar Panickar.

(x) D.D. Kosambi: D.D. Kosambi was a great scholar and versatile historian. His mind was fresh and original. In fact it was a mathematical mind working on historical problems and therefore he could be as stimulating as Plato or a Russell. Frankly he was a Marxist.

No doubt he was a reputed mathematician in the beginning of his career. Then he turned towards history. His contributions are very interesting and stimulating to the readers. They are:

(1) Introduction to the study of Indian History.

(2) Culture and civilisation of ancient India in historical outline.

(3) Myth and Reality in Indian History.

The above works are considered as the most important of his contributions to history.

D.D. Kosambi lay special emphasis on archaeology and anthropology as necessary pre requisites of a historian's equipment. He is intolerant of romantic history, in fact, of any history other than analytical. To him Gita is a feudal document. He has said unsavoury things about Gita. His approach to history is like that of Marx in very many aspects. In this way he has given new phrases of history.

(xi) R.C. Majumdar: R.C. Majumdar was born in 1888. He was educated at Calcutta where he obtained the Ph. D degree. He had a brilliant academic career. He became professor of history at the Calcutta University and Vice Chancellor of Dacca University. He wrote many books. They are:

(1) Corporate Life in Ancient India.

(2) History of Bengal.

(3) Advanced History of India.

(4) The History and Culture of the Indian People.

R.C. Majumdar's Advanced History of India was written in collaboration with Roy Chaudhuri and Datta. It has been a useful and standard text book covering the whole of the History of India. His editorship of the eleven volume. History of India (The History and Culture of the Indian People) sponsored by K.M. Munshi's Bharatiya Vidya Bhavan. His Heras memorial lectures on Historiography in Modern India comprising not more than sixty pages summarises his views on the art of writing history. His History of Freedom Movement is a controversial one.

He has been president of the All India History Congress and the All India Oriental Conference. He was the Vice-President of the international commission set up by the UNESCO for editing the history of mankind.

20

Theological Interpretation of History

Generally the historian is not satisfied with more facts about the past. But he is interested in finding about what caused these events to take place and attempts to explain the significance of the facts. Some events are classified as historical facts. It is the primary duty of the historian to explain and interpret them in such a way as to appreciate the past. Hence, mere collection of facts, does not constitute history. The task of interpretation has to be taken in the light of some accepted norm which would add sense and meaning to his labours. Unless the story of mankind is interpreted and told in a convincing manner nobody would be interested in the study of the past. However, this problem of interpretation is beset with some difficulties.

Historian and His Facts

According to E.H. Carr there is continuous process of interaction between the historian and his facts. He has to answer the problems convincingly. "Why did the great civilisations of the past decline in course of time?" How did the foreigners, time and again manage to invade India? What contributed to the rise of Mughal Power? How did Napoleon Bonaparte reach the pinnacle of glory? Countless questions can be based on the known facts and the historian is bound to give reasonable explanation of the events.

Necessity of Interpretation: There is no sense in choosing to study history without explanations and interpretations for the sake of merely studying about past men whose actions and ideas are not clear, whose motives are obscure and whose significance is lost to the posterity or is unintelligible. Only by interpretation he lights up the stage of human past and transforms the dead dummies and mummies into vibrant figures conveying a sense of purpose and unity of them. No doubt it can be possible only by interpretation of the past.

Theological Interpretation: It is considered as one of the most important views on interpretation. By this outlook, human actions are considered as motivated by Divine Will. It is believed that there must be some reason for all that had happened in the past. God created the whole universe and everything takes place by His Dispensation. This conception of the past has been advocated from time immemorial and has its adherents even in modern times. Some problems are attributed to Divine Will, since they are difficult to answer. Generally great historians believe in Divine Will. So history was treated as co-ordinate with the purpose of creation.

Difficulties in explanation: Theological interpretation sets up psychological and emotional barriers. Violence and bloodshed occurred due to the clash of rival groups on religious basis. Meaningless wars, the suffering of innocent people due to exploitation, wastage of men and materials in destructive activities and the rest are explained with great difficulty. When there is a clash between Christianity and Islam or between Islam and Hinduism how is the success of one party at a particular juncture and of the other at a different juncture to be explained and interpreted. This kind of explanation leads to philosophical speculations on the nature of man, universe and God. The historian should be interested in discovering and explaining human factors and not take shelter under the shade of theological values.

It cannot be denied that religion Eastern or Western has played a very significant part in moulding human character and values.

Secular Interpretation

History is very much concerned with the past events. Human aspirations and failures are, then, to be assessed, from human point of view. Every human action is destined to divine dispensation. The interpretation of history through the medium of human understanding frees the historian from religious preconditions. The draw of the past is sought to be explained and interpreted to present from human angles. This gives greater elbow room for the historian to scrutinise the events and plausible causes. The historian in trying to understand the past also understands the present in a more meaningful way. The perils of early voyages of discovery, the fearlessness in landing upon unknown continents after chartering the turbulent oceans raises in the hearts of the present a thrill and pride in the adventurous spirit of human beings. At the same time the follies of the past, the obstacles in the form of ignorance and prejudice, shake off the present to strive for great attainments. In short the historian is able to survey the past and present events though perils and pleasures.

In his "Studying History, How and Why?" Daniels brings out the role of time dimension in these words: "The most distinctive feature of the historical approach of course is its emphasis on the time dimension. This forces as to look at the present as the product of the past, and also as a transitory point in an on going evolutionary process..............."

In this connection certain modern interpretations have been given on this point. The age of Renaissance and Reformation unleashed forms of free intellectual approach to the problems of the past. The Revolution of 1789 in France and its aftermath and the Marxian approach in economic interpretation made substantial change in the outlook of interpretations.

Thus the great historians in their attempt to interpret the past and narrate the course of mankind's history developed their own ideas about different stages in man's civilised life, the agencies responsible for bringing about changes in the pattern of life.

21

Historical Determinism

Determinism and Free Will: Historical determinism is a doctrine which postulates that the historical process *i.e.*, the entirety of it, is predetermined or pre-destined. The events of the past took place in the way it did because they had been ordained accordingly and that no other forms of action were possible or even desirable. This determinism would explain the causes of events in the light of mankind submitting to a higher will than its own or in the case of materialistic interpretations, even purely on the basis of material explanations suggesting that they had to happen in the chalked out way. Man's actions are the results of his own volition and the course of events depend upon his sagacity, judgement, capacity and suitability to the times. The individual will act according to the best of his judgement and there is no need to invoke the blessings of a higher power.

The most important manifestation of historical determinism is economic determinism. This theory is best summarised by Engels in his 'Anti Duhring.' The determinist explanation of history may take on either metaphysical kind of Hegel or materialistic kind of Marx. In the case of Hegelian doctrine the process of unfolding the past ended with the explanation and its significance to the present while Marx did not hesitate to anticipate a course for the future in the light of the past material struggles. The will of Hegel did not go beyond the prescriptions of the established routine and meek submission to the Reason while Marxian dogmas direct the 'Specific class of people to realise that the future is theirs and instill in them a sense to hasten the end.'

According to E.H. Carr, "Like the ordinary man, historian believes that human actions have causes which are in principle ascertainable. History, like everybody life, would be impossible if this assumption were not made. It is the special function of historian to investigate these causes. This may be to give him a special interest in the determined aspect of human behaviour, but he does not reject free will except on the untenable hypothesis that voluntary actions have no cause......As a historian, I am perfectly prepared to do without 'inevitable', 'unavoidable', 'in escapable' and even 'incalculable'.

The problem of determinism and free will, therefore, has to be understood not only in the light of historical perspective but along, philosophical and sociological grounds as well. Page Smith estimating Hegelian role in the Romantic Idealistic period states, "The German philosopher presented to a responsive audience a notion of history as the progressive development of reason through God's providence. Man's spirit, made lip of nature and the divine Idea, was fulfilled in history."

Historictsm: Historicism originally meant 'development and continuity' as fundamental characteristics of the historical process, and is connected with the German word "Historismus". Friedrich and Meinecke Use the word to mean the rise of a new historical outlook to denote the vital importance of intellectual history in the study of the developments of nation and culture.

Grace gives another meaning to the word, namely, the science of history. He says that the "ideas or values which have been taken as the measure and the methods of history are not universal ideas and values. But are themselves particular and historical facts elevated to the rank of universals".

Barraclough said that 'historicism is the old progenitor of relativism.' He says that "as in historicism, in relativism also truth about a situation is sought to be understood in terms of relation to its context, environment, antecedents etc." and not admitting of situations external values and actions. According to this definition historicism asserts that there are no absolutes".

Burckhardt said that 'history signifies only relativism.' One of those who made fundamental contributions to this idea of relativism was Wilhem Dilthey (1833-1911).

K.P. Popper is the greatest and the most logical opponent of the doctrine of historicism. According to him 'it is the task of the social sciences to propound historical prophecies and historical prophecies are needed if we wish to conduct politics in a rational way.'

Page Smith calls relativism as a step child to Hegelianism. He does not believe in objective history and while ascribing high moral value to history tends to regard views on humanist or secular outlook of historical studies as banal. In short relativism severely restricts the scope of historical investigations.

A careful study of the past would undoubtedly teach many valuable lessons. Only extreme views by thinkers like Nietzsche denying objection would detract the merit of history.

Relativism implies interpretation of past events in the proper perspective of the age. The same set of facts can be viewed from different angles by historians. We should remember that even though values and view points differ from age to age, there are certain permanent values which are recognised by the ages. Though the historians try to be objective, one cannot rule out subjective element creeping in from time to time as the historians are also conditioned by the age in which they live in. Moreover the logic of events sometimes may puzzle the historian living at a later time.

We must also reject the relativist view that since there can be no absolute judgements and values different interpretations and judgements may be considered right in their own way. This type of reasoning would not only lead all sorts of interpretations and no change and purposeful study of the past can be undertaken. E.H. Carr rightly points out, "when economic and social ends began to replace constitutional and political ends, historians turn to economic and social interpretations of the past. Moreover he says that the old interpretation is not rejected, but is both included and superseded in the new."

22

Research in History

(1) Selection of Topic for Research

Historical knowledge can be widened only by constant and careful research work. G.R. Elton (The Practice of History) very beautifully sums up the scope of historical research in these words. "Historical method is no more than a recognised and tested way of extracting from what the past has left the true facts and events of that past, and so far as possible their true meaning and interrelation, the whole governed by the first principle of historical understanding, namely that the past must be studied in its own right, for its own sake and on its own terms. It is a way of turning the evidence to account and though there is nothing mysterious about it, it is nevertheless vigorous and not to be confused with the so called common sense approach of the intelligent but untutored enthusiast. If fundamental principles are only two, and they may be expressed as questions thus exactly what evidence is there, and exactly what does it mean?" From this we know the scope of historical research very clearly. Many factors are to be carefully considered and proper attention paid to the selection of topic for research.

According to Robert V. Daniels, "The basic difference between the creative artist and the historian is the source of the latter's material. It comes not from imagination and personal experience but from study — the study of the written records of the past, in other words, historical research."

It must be obvious that research is calculated to extend the frontiers of knowledge in regard to any area of intellectual pursuit. This may be wide or narrow, may relate to new discovery, an invention, a point of view, a new arrangement, a new proof and so forth based upon existing data or marshalling of hitherto unknown data.

Research involves original planning if the thesis is a new breakthrough at the theoretical and speculative level and if it is to be brilliant and valuable. Nothing else can constitute research.

Research by proxy is no research. The historical architect must 'quarry his own stones and build with his own hands' says G.M. Trevelyan.

It should be borne in mind that research is the basics for establishing history.

Basic requisites: In order to embark upon a project of research work the scholar should have certain basic mental attitudes.

(i) He should be free from bias and prejudices.

(ii) He should think in terms of ascertaining all the possible facts from primary or secondary sources.

(iii) He should be zealous in gathering as much facts as possible.

(iv) He should be objective.

(v) He should make a fair interpretation.

(vi) He should carefully consider the learned opinions on the already known facts but pronounce his own verdict without being weighed down by the way of other authorities on the subject.

(vii) He should be a creative artist in the subject concerned.

The choice of topic: Now the scholar is confronted with the problem of choosing a topic for research. He must choose his topic with reference to 1. his own predilections and 2. the facilities for research on the subject available to him. In this process the supervisor can help the scholar in choosing his topic.

Choice of topic will not be an easy task for having initially chosen a topic, he may soon discover that it does not work either because there is no material on it or it is not philosophically self-contained. Before he wastes more time on it he must change his topic.

It is very obvious that the viability of the topic above will depend on only two factors, availability of material and sufficiency of the subject. In addition to this intelligence and industry is very essential to pursue the research. When he has finally chosen the subject he would have tested if for problems *i.e.*, whether he can collect sufficient facts for generalisation and whether the topic will yield problems for investigation. So everyone with these basic qualifications can pursue research; and the words of Kitson Clark. "No scholar holds monopoly rights on any historical subject whatsoever" are relevant.

Before choosing a subject it would be preferable for a student to check up whether the topic has already been worked upon. To avoid repetitive work, topic banks and clearing houses of research subject should be set up. Different scholars can work the same subject in different ways.

The selection of topic should make the scholar realise the greatness of the task ahead of him. He should take up a theme of manageable proportion and endeavour to do full justice to the theme. In the early stages of research career he would do well to explore a theme with limited frame work so that he understands the difficulties and problems of research. He should begin with modest aims. In short research is almost a way of life and the sooner one learns the technique of correct appraisal the better for him.

The choice of topic involves its definition and delimitation, compact neat little topics like, for example, the Kadavarayas in the later Chola period or the Great Temple Tanjore can be worked upon. In the second stage we have to deal with the matter very carefully. So the scholar should define his area of work stating whether he is going to be concerned with the art and architecture of the temple or the history of its construction or its role in the socio-economic life of the people etc. This kind of delimitation of every subject is desirable before it is taken up for research. Delimitation would relate to space and time.

Collection and Selection of Facts

The scholar is beset with the problem of collecting and selecting facts regarding his topic whether it is narrower or wider in theme. In either case he will find a huge amount of source material to be carefully arranged, selected and probed into. The first and foremost duty of a research scholar is to know how to locate the source material. Secondly he should not trust his memory alone for immediately locating particular source material. Moreover the research scholar should be armed with appropriate aids to stand by his study in his voyage of discovery.

According to learned authorities the research scholars should keep a file of 3”× 5” cards. As soon as the researcher consults a source material he must make a brief note of the reference in the card indicating the purpose for which it is consulted.

Arrangement of cards with appropriate remarks will go a long way in easing the burden of the researcher later on. Separate card for each item of reference is necessary.

The name of the source material, its particular necessity, even page numbers of the books etc., will help the scholar considerably.

Apart from the bibliographical and index cards of the libraries the research scholar should prepare and keep his own set of cards.

Additional references should be noted if they are related to his area of interest. Separate cards for each source material should be indicated.

The Art of Selection: Auxiliary science like archaeology, numismatics, epigraphy, chronology etc., are immensely useful for history. History is aided by those sciences. With great patience he should learn to select from the multitude of material suitable for his purpose. The general rule is that he must be familiar with all the sources available.

A scholar should be very particular with primary sources not with secondary sources. He should consult only the primary sources for his research topic.

Conclusion: According to Turner the materials available to the historians are immensely useful. Every source is valuable to them. But the researcher should be cautious about the choice of his topic and appropriate material which he can use for his enquiry. Mere accumulation of facts will not do. He should strive for deciphering a meaning; a pattern into the maze of facts available for him sometimes conflicting and contradictory too and earnestly attempt to interpret the facts.

The scholar, in the early stages of his career itself, need not wait till the collection of all the facts for analysis and writing. He can begin the writing almost from the early stages and proceed to enlarge the argument. He must pose questions and problems and in the light of his own observation and understanding arrive at the conclusion without fear or favour.

The research scholar should aim at arriving at truth without bias and aided by objectivity.

Proper attention should be paid to his style of writing and manner of putting forth his arguments effectively. Good style cannot be construed as history. It is better and fitter to conclude with Daniel, "Research is the keystone of historical study, for the student it is the most difficult and demanding aspect of the subject but also the most rewarding in the interest and training it affords."

(2) Sources of Historical Writing

Ancient: The historian reconstructs the past from the available evidence left behind by man in his evolutionary march. The historian weaves his tapestry by various sources like the cities he lived in, the articles and weapons that he used, the monuments, sculptures, bronzes, paintings and other works of art he created, the thoughts and feelings of man enshrined in the literary works, artistic contributions and the institutions of man etc.

There was no great historian in ancient India; hence there was no written history. In the words of Alberuni, "The Hindus do not pay much attention to the historical order of things; they are very careless in relating the chronological succession of their kings, and when they are pressed for information and are at a loss, not knowing what to say, they invariably take to tale-telling."

Fleet observes thus "It is very questionable whether the ancient Hindus ever possessed the pure historical sense, in the shape of the faculty of putting together genuine history on broad and critical lines."

No doubt there existed a vast amount of historical writings of various kinds. In that the sources of ancient history of India are unlimited in number.

The above sources can be divided into two divisions. They are:

(i) archaeological sources and

(ii) literary sources.

Archaeological sources consists of monuments, works of art, inscriptions and coins.

The literary works are mostly works of tradition, contemporary chronicles and accounts left by the foreigners.

"Archaeology is the study of man made antiquities and so it is history approached from study of the surviving objects of the past."

Archaeological sources for the ancient history are available plenty in number. In 1861 the British government established the Archaeological Survey of India. Brilliant men like Cunningham, Burgess and John Marshall did a lot for the same. They have unearthed many historical findings of great importance. They have excavated the historic places like Nalanda, Samath, Rajagriha, Sanchi and Kushinagara. Historical cities like Patliputra and Taxila revealed the details of dynastic history. The momentous discovery of the Indus Valley Civilisation pushed back the history of India by two thousand years.

Inscriptions have rendered invaluable help for the reconstruction of the ancient history of India. It is very difficult to establish any definite date and identification without the help of inscriptions. The materials used for engraving the inscriptions were clay, copper, bronze, gold, silver, brass and iron. The languages normally used in the inscriptions were Pali, Tamil, Sanskrit, Prakrit, Telugu, Kannada and Malayalam. The popular script that was used in these inscriptions was Brahmi. It was written from left to right. Another script was Kharoshti that was written from right to left.

Some inscriptions are commemorative; some are dedicatory; some are donative. The commemorative and dedicatory inscriptions comprise a vast variety normally ranging from an indication of a name to an elaborate poem, composed in splendid style. They are usually recorded on stone. The donative inscriptions are indications of grants; they are mostly recorded on copper plates.

We get a lot of informations about political, social and economic history of ancient times from the inscriptions. The following are concrete examples for the same:

(a) The seals of Harappa and Mohenjodaro,

(b) Edicts of Asoka,

(c) The inscriptions of the Mauryas,

(d) The inscriptions of the Cholas,

(e) The inscriptions of the Pallavas and the Pandyas.

The Rummaindei Inscriptions refer Asoka's visit to Lumbini which has also helped the scholars to locate the birth place of the Buddha.

The Allahabad Pillar Inscriptions of Samudra Gupta provide information regarding the achievements of the ruler.

The Uttaramerur Inscription helps us to have an idea about the working of local self-government in the Tamil country during ancient times.

The Leyden grant of Rajaraja and the Tiruvalangadu plates of the great Rajendra Chola provide invaluable information about the Chola Kings.

Coins are the important source of information for the historians. Hoard of coins have been unearthed by private individuals in different places. The discovery of large quantities of Roman coins in Arikamedu is a noteworthy example of the commercial connection between South India and the mighty Roman Empire. The symbols, figures and legends on coins throw light on the administration of the country.

The earliest coins were punch-marked coins. They are called so because of the peculiar method of punching the symbols on the face of the coins. They provide information for the history of major as well as small powers.

Traditions, chronicles and foreign accounts furnish a lot of historical information. Kural, Silappathikaram, the Jatahas, the Vedas and the Upanishads are principal works of tradition.

Among the chronicles, the genealogical tables and biographies are worthy to be mentioned. The Rajatarangini of Kalhana and Bana's Harshacharita are best examples for chronicles.

Foreign accounts are available to the historians to reconstruct the ancient history of India. The accounts of Megasthenes (Indica) Fahien, Yuan Chuang and Itsing are immensely useful to us. Fahien gives a glowing picture of the rule of Chandragupta Vikramaditya. Yuan Chuang visited India and gives a vivid picture of India in his account. "Their accounts are a mine of information on the social and cultural aspects of the life of the times. It is true they viewed life mainly from the Buddhist angle but still our understanding is deepened by their accounts."

Medieval: The sources for the Medieval Period of Indian History are available in plenty.

According to K.A.N. Sastri, "The historians of this period of Indian History possess marked advantage over the scholars interested in the preceding period.

Archaeological Sources: Generally the Muslim rulers were great patrons of arts. They built numerous forts, palaces and other works of art. Qutb-Minar, started by Qutb-ud-din was completed by Iltutmish, is regarded as a tower of victoiy. It is considered as the best monument of their period.

The city of Siri, Tughlakabad, Firazabad and other buildings throw light upon the architectural styles of the period.

Hindu monuments like the pillar of victory erected by Rana Kumbha at Chittor and the Vittala Temple built by Krishna Deva Raya are standing examples.

Fatehpur Sikri, the Mughal gardens and the Taj Mahal are best examples for the Mughal architecture.

Besides from Mughal paintings we get a lot of information regarding their life and activities.

Literary Sources: A large number of chroniclers contributed much on the rules of the Delhi Sultanate and the Mughal Empire.

Minaj-us-Siraj wrote Tabakati Nasiri, a general history of the Muslim world.

Barani's Tarikh-i-Firoz Shahi is the history of the Delhi Sultanate from Balban to the 6th regional year of Firuz Shah Tughlaq.

Amir Khusrau's (the Prince of Poets and the Parrot of Hind) Khazain-ul-Futuh is the important source of information for the period of Ala-ud-din Khilji.

Sultan Firuz Shah Tughlaq's Futuhat-i-Firuz Shahi provides information on his administration.

For the history of the Lodis the works of Ahmad Yadgar, Nimatullah and Abdullah are immensely useful.

Babur's Memoirs provides a lot of information about India of that period. In his Memoirs or autobiography, Babur gave vivid description of Hindustan.

Gulbadan Begum, Babur's daughter wrote Humayun Nama which throws flood of light into the life of the Mughal harem.

Abul Fazl's works on the administration of Akbar, Aini Akbari and Akbarnama are best sources of the period.

Badauni's Muntakhab-ul-Tawarikh deals with the history of Hindustan from Sabaktigin to Akbar. He criticised Akbar without any fear Or favour.

Tabaqat-i-Akbari composed by Khwaja Nizamuddin refers to the history of the Muslim powers in India.

The Memoirs of Jahangir is another equally important source of information on Mughal history.

Padshah-Nama of Abdul Hamid and Alamgir Nama of Muhammad Kazim and Khafi Khan's Muntakhab-ul-Lubab are very important sources of the Mughal period.

Foreign Sources: The writings of foreign travellers and merchants who visited and resided in the Mughal court are also the best sources of information concerning the Mughal period. Arab chroniclers and Islamic historians gave much importance to the development in India in medieval times and left behind them invaluable accounts.

Alberuni, the great Arabic scholar wrote a comprehensive work on India.

Ibn-Batuta lived in India for several years and his account of Muhammad-bin-Tughluq is a valuable supplement to the indigeneous sources.

The Italian Nicolo Conti, the Persian ambassador Abdur Razzak, the Russian trader Athanasius Nikitin and other foreign visitors have given beautiful account of Vijayanagar Empire.

The Jesuit missionaries, Captain Hawkins, Sir Thomas Roe, the French travellers like Bernier and Tavernier have given a pen picture of the Mughal period. Their diaries and travel accounts gave us an invaluable source of information regarding the political, economic and social conditions of the people.

Modern: The sources for the history of modern India are available in plenty. Literary sources are the main information.

Ever since their arrival in India the European powers, the Portuguese, the Dutch, the French and the English based their transactions in India on State Papers. Then they established their supremacy. After that they took keen interest in preserving the documents.

The English East India Company kept every detailed written records of their transactions for their perusal of their masters.

The British preserved the notes, letters and other papers of Madras, Bombay and Calcutta presidencies very carefully during their rule. These are very helpful to the historians to reconstruct the history of modern India.

Moreover they created the Imperial Record Offices at New Delhi and India Office at London. The second mentioned office alone contains more than 50 thousand volumes in its records collection. "It is an inspiring centre of research and many historians have availed themselves of the facilities which are generally provided by the authorities of the departments."

After Independence, the record offices were reorganised into state archives. The State Archives at Madras, Calcutta and Bombay possess the largest collections of the records and documents pertaining to the British Indian history.

The Imperial Records office is now a days called the National Archives, situated in Delhi.

There are some important records preserved by individuals in the land. They are very useful for historical writers.

The Portuguese, the Dutch, the French and the Danes had their strong holds at Goa, Nagapatnam, Pondicherry and Tarangambadi respectively. The Portuguese had their archives at Lisbon, and Nova Goa. The Dutch archives preserved valuable papers and records. The French Records at Pondicherry provide information on the administration of the French settlements in India like Pondicherry, Karaikal and Mahe.

Besides the foreign sources, the following Indian sources are available in different languages.

1. The Marathi historical records were published by the Bombay Government itself in 1934 in 45 Volumes edited by G.S. Sardesai under the title of 'Selections from the Peshwas Daftar.'
2. J.N. Sarkar has edited some of the Persian sources under the title "The Persian Sources of Maratha History" in 1953
3. Papers on Hydrabad principality.
4. Papers available on the principalities of Travancore and Coorg.

Apart from the above sources there are chronicles, diaries, travel accounts and historical sketches. For example the Persian work Siyur-ul Mutakharin provides information on the conditions in India in the 18th century. The Diary of Ananda Rangam Pillai Dubash to Francois Dupleix, written in Tamil is a voluminous source of information providing information on the nature of Anglo-French relations, the social customs and the personality of that great statesman. Dubois, the French missionary wrote a very invaluable work, 'Hindu Manners, Customs and Ceremonies.' Buchanan produced an account of his travel from Madras to Mysore and Malabar.

In addition to the above sources the following historical works are of great contemporary value:

1. History of British India by James Mill.
2. H.T. Princep's History of the Political and Military Transactions in India during the Administration of the Marques of Hastings.'
3. J.W. Kaye's History of the war in Afghanistan.
4. History of the Marathas by Grant Duff.
5. Mark Wilk's History of Mysore.
6. J.D. Cunningham's History of the Sikhs.

Apart from the written works, there are journals, periodicals and dailies to provide historical information.

The following sources provide some information to historical writers:

1. Lord Curzon's works.
2. Robert's '41 years in India'.
3. S.N. Banerjea's 'A Nation in the Making'.
4. Edwin Montague's 'An Indian Diary.'
5. Pattabi Sita Ramaiah's 'The History of Indian National Congress.'
6. Babu Rajendra Prasad's 'India Divided.'
7. S. Gopal's 'The Viceroyalty of Lord Ripon.'
8. The works of W.W. Hunter, Sir Alfred Lyall and Sir Richard Temple.
9. A.B. Keith's 'Indian Constitutional History.'

Thus we have abundant sources for the modern period.

(3) Collection of Data: (Refer this chapter)

(4) Objectivity in Writing History

Objectivity is very essential in historical writing. But the very nature of history which is neither scientific nor mechanical makes it extremely difficult to have a completely objective history. It is said that "completely objective and dispassionate history is an illusion". Moreover there is a bias in the choice of the topic, selection of material, in its organisation and presentation. Historians are creatures of their time, their race, their faith, their class, their country. Since history is the record of the past and a record implies a recorder, whose views and convictions will enter his record. Hence we cannot have a totally objective history.

To begin with, it is necessary to know the meanings of the words; objective and subjective. First, objective means 'the mental state or quality of being objective', it also means 'the external reality.' Objective is deviced from object which is a reality external to the mind; therefore it is not mere thought on cognition, invention, intention, imagination, feeling, sensitivity etc., all of which are personal to the mind, inward and subjective. These ideas, feelings, emotions, loves and hates are called subjective because they belong entirely to and emanate from the subject that is the person whose mind is experiencing these emotive feelings. The subject is the self. Everything outside it or external to it is object.

Herodotus and Voltaire tried their best to make history objective. Ranke and his school of historians asserted the necessity of objectivity in historical writing. But perfect objectivity can never be achieved.

Historical objectivity, makes one to understand what is true and real. It means the state of being free from personal bias and sentimental approach, personal and partial. In order to understand the real value of history it is to be written objectively.

History can be treated as science and hence it reveals the truth as it is. But history has to present itself objectively. It should be impersonal, impartial and capable of experimentation.

Moreover history is not a science like that of physical science. The objectivity arrived at by the historian is not the same as that of the scientist. Yet objectivity should be arrived in historical writing.

Further objectivity is essential in order to avoid different accounts—sometimes very conflicting views of the same, each writer forms a particular point of view. "The events of — 1857 have been described from many angles and termed ask a Mutiny, revolt, rebellion, sepoy war, Indian war of Independence etc." There are about three hundred works on the subject and they vary widely in the degree of "objectivity obtained."

Historians recognised the importance of objectivity. At the same time it becomes difficult when put into practice. Historians rarely agree on what really happened. That is mainly due to tastes, prejudices and commitments of the historical writers. In the opinion of G.M. Trevelyan, "when one writes, he is present in his work with his whole personality, with his temperament with his reason and with his group consciousness."

We can cite many examples in history to show the fact that historians have not done full justice to the historical characters and themes. Such an eminent historian Gibbon too failed to appreciate the role of the Byzantine Empire. He could not show it to the public that it was the centre of culture and prosperity.

T.B. Macaulay while glorifying the Glorious Revolution of 1688 could not appreciate the good work of William III.

Lord Acton hoped that new generations of historians could be in a position to write an objective history in a good manner.

History is selective. A historian can highlight only certain aspects of a theme and not give an exhaustive account of it. There are certain factors which make one to disagree. Personal prejudice is one of the important factors influencing any historical work.

But personal likes and dislikes are not so harmful as long as fundamental factors are not trusted and turned to achieve a preconceived pattern. The contemporary accounts by the British writers were not free from personal prejudice may be due to race, religion and nationalism. V.D. Savarkar wrote the "First war of Independence" with a determination to strengthen the patriotic forces in India and to embarrass Great Britain. The French disregarded the battles of Blenheim, Ramillies, Oudenarde and Malplaquet in the war of Spanish Succession in their accounts. But the English students are given full details about them in their books written by their historians.

Besides, there are other factors like ignorance, fear and motivation to do so or to write perverted history. Some major developments may be ignored by the historians due to paucity of sources. Gibbon's treatment of the Byzantine Empire can be cited as a classical example. The court historians like Ferishta and Abul Fazl wrote history in order to satisfy their self interests.

No doubt the historical writers strive hard to attain objectivity in their writtings. Of course it is desirable but not attainable.

So far an attempt has been made to analyse the possibility of history being objective. But due to intervention of inevitable factors, history cannot be objective. History is subjective only. According to Robert V. Daniels "Objectivity is of course essential in historical research. This does not mean giving up all your opinions and values — that would not be human. What objectivity means in practice is the ability to face facts, whether you like them or not. It is particularly important in facing unfavourable facts about people or institutions that you have endorsed because you thought that they represented your values."

(5) Heuristic

According to K.A.N. Sastri, "the historical method embodies within itself a body of rules which each researcher should follow when he undertakes work on any problem of history." In other words, historical method deals with the complicated operations of criticism, and construction of analysis and synthesis.

The German historians realised the importance of the study of historical method in the 19th century. They were the first people to do so. The great German historian Ranke and his pupils were the pioneers to apply these principles to historical research. But they did not write any treatise on method. Bamheim the foremost writer on historical method contributed a comprehensive treatise on the subject. "It is the first detailed and scientific presentation of the processes of historical investigation and has been the guide of the generations of scholars and historians."

Another important work in this field was "Introduction to the Study of History" by Langlois and Seignobos written in French. It was translated into English by G.C. Berry.

Then came the celebrated work "History, Its Method and Purpose" by the Dutch scholar Renier. He has fairly dealt with the various problems of methodology giving much importance to Philosophy of History.

There are four parts in the historical method. They are:

(1) Heuristics

(2) Criticism

(3) Synthesis and

(4) Exposition.

The four divisions exactly correspond to the main duties of the historian.

Heuristics deals with the art of search for and the collection of various kinds of documents. In other words this process of identification of the sources is known as Heuristics. The historian or the research scholar should know the exact places of localities where the documents are lying.

The second function of the historian is to critically interpret or examine the collected facts, known as criticism.

The third function is to group the historical facts and to ascertain their casual genesis, technically known as 'synthesis'.

The last duty of methodology is the narration or the presentation of the historical facts referred as 'exposition.'

Heuristics, the first part is the art of searching for and the collection of various documents which form the main sources of history. Heuristics derived from the German word 'Heuristik' means to find out things. Documents are very essential for research. They are found in various forms. They are:

(1) Monuments

(2) Sculptures

(3) Paintings

(4) Pottery

(5) Coins

(6) Tradition

(7) Speeches

Archaeological evidence is very essential for ancient Indian History.

The Central Archaeological Department of India and the State Departments have done good service in the preservation and collection of these various monuments, sculptures, inscriptions and coins. The National Archives of India and similar state organisations (particularly Madras and Bombay) are doing great service in preserving the various records of the modern period. Here one has to take care of the unpublished records also. Any research scholar intend doing research on any aspect of ancient Indian histoiy should go through the various reports of Archaeological Survey of India and the reports of State Archaeological Departments.

There are mainly two kinds of sources primary and secondary. Primary sources relate to contemporary material on the subject like the Tuzuk-i-Jahangiri being primary material for the history of the reign of Jahangir.

Secondary sources are like Ferishta's History of Early Medieval India, basing himself upon earlier sources. Inscriptions, accounts provided by eye witnesses, narratives on travels and records of Government belong to this category of primary sources. In spite of the availability of sources, research scholars find it difficult to locate them. They have to refer the index to inscriptions, guides to record, calanders to periodicals, who's who, library catalogues and hand books. According to K.A.N. Sastri "Heuristics forms the first and foremost part of the historian's craft without which he cannot proceed with further work and investigation."

(6) Criticism — Internal and External

It is very essential that a researcher should test the validity of the evidence supporting his thesis. This testing is called criticism.

Generally criticism shall be confined to an enquiry about the relationship between the evidence and the thesis.

In this test irrelevant evidence, if it is not prima facie shall be rejected. This does not mean that the rejected evidence is either absolutely false or is useless for all purposes. It only means that it is useless for the purpose on hand. To put it in a nut shell criticism is not the end and aim of historical research.

Broadly speaking the process of criticism falls into two parts: 1. external criticism and 2. internal criticism. These two modes of historical criticism constitute the central part of research in the writing of history.

External Criticism

External criticism determines the degree of authenticity of documents. It examines whether a particular document or a relic is genuine or not. In his "Critical Method in Historical Research and Writing" H.C. Hockett says that "external criticism is of a lower type and includes examination of documents like manuscripts, books, pamphlets, maps including ancient inscriptions and monuments, "with a view to obtain all possible information of any significance about their origin and if need be of restoring the original form of writing."

In the opinion of Langlois and Seignobos, "External criticism means the first group of preliminary investigations, bearing upon the writing, the form, the source."

External criticism deals with the authorship of documents, the source, handwriting, dates, the question of genuineness, purity etc. Paleography, archaeology and chronology are used to determine the genuineness of a document. Hence a historian should be well versed with the above aids.

But the work of external criticism is mainly preliminary. It studies only the outside form of the documents. It identifies the author of the document, determines its age with the help of the various auxiliary sciences. At the same time, the internal value of the document must be studied. The process by which the trustworthiness of the document is studied, is generally known as 'Internal criticism'.

According to Langlois and Seignobos, "Internal criticism endeavours, by the help of analogies mostly borrowed from general psychology, to reproduce the mental states through which the author of the document passed." In short the research scholar must try to analyse the contents of the real meaning. In the words of Heras, "the object of internal criticism is to disclose what in a document may be accepted as true. It has also been called 'hermeneutics.'

Internal criticism is really essential to a researcher, because many of the documents were without adequate knowledge; mostly they were written with motivation or prejudice. During the early times the court historians and modern writers have written history with prejudice, bias and partiality. Sometimes it so happens that the historians in spite of knowing the truth, they are not in a position to record "what had actually happened"— for fear of consequences. The British administrators also followed their own bias in writing the events. It is the duty of a research scholar to scrutinise the same fairly. Thus internal criticism deals with the contents of the documents, their probability, author's veracity etc.

Internal Criticism contains two parts:

1. Positive interpretative criticism and 2. Negative criticism.

Positive interpretative criticism analyses the contents of the document with a view to its truth. Whenever the document is in the form of writing, both the literal and real meaning must be determined. Moreover the researcher must have a thorough study of the text itself. It helps the researcher to understand the motive of the author. Thus he understands the real meaning of the document.

Negative Criticism. Here a researcher should look at the document with a view to identify the errors, the negative elements, so that they can be eliminated.

The researcher should not accept the views, theories and statements of the early writers at their face value and should take them only as presumptions till they are verified and proved as correct. All that cannot be proved must be temporarily regarded as doubtful. It may be due to two reasons: (1) The author may not be in a position to tell the truth. (2) He may not have ability to tell truth eventhough he may sincerely try to tell the truth. In otherwords, the good faith of the author is verified in the first while in the second the accuracy of the author is tested. They are called errors of good faith and errors of accuracy. In brief the author's entire psychology or the mental make up has to be very seriously studied.

Of course criticism is not an easy task. "Criticism is above all else a gift, an intuition, a matter of tact and flair. It cannot be taught or demonstrated. It is an art."

The different ways of criticism can be easily followed with the help of a chart:

CRITICISM

- External Criticism
- Internal Criticism
  - Positive Interpretative Criticism
  - Negative Criticism

The above facts clearly indicate the importance of criticism in the writing of history.

(7) Synthesis and Interpretation

Synthesis and interpretation go together without discovering an overall meaning for the thesis, the scholar cannot synthesise the material to secure a personality for it. Interpretation involves the recognition of problems pertaining to the thesis and later discovering appropriate or at least credible solution for them. To be able to see a problem is the index of a scholar's original intellectual gift. He must be able to frame questions and that is possible only for the learned. The questions must be relevant, precise and pointed. The first question is a basic question from which further questions can stem. A series of connected questions should be able to scan the length and breadth of the thesis. Problems are different from simple questions. They are of much greater dimensions and more fundamental.

Synthesis is the art of organising the mass of material that has been finally accepted for use in the thesis. The thesis begins with a hypothesis, introduces the core of the thesis in a preliminary introduction, lists and criticises the source material, divides the mass of historical material into convenient parts either chronologically or thematically and at the end puts in a concluding chapter in which whatever has gone before is summarised and the scholarly achievement put in proper perspective.

The most popular criteria for the arrangement of historical data is that of chronology. Gardiner wrote his seventeenth century history according to strict chronological order and did not attach importance to the history of the subsequent year unless he had completed the study of the previous year.

V.A. Smith's 'Akbar the Great Mughal' is based mainly on the chronological basis.

Macaulay holds that the chronological arrangement produces notoriously unreadable history.

Jacques Barzan and Henry F. Graff in their book "The Modern Researcher" point out that the strict chronological order mixes events great and small without due subordination and that it combines incidents that occupy only once with permanent truths about habits and tastes, character and belief; it is a parody of life.

Historical material can also be arranged on the basis of the subject instead of time. This kind of arrangement is known as topical approach. The first volume of the Cambridge History of India is based on various topics. However, in this method there is always possibility that the historian may lose the fundamental historical essence of change through time. In the opinion of Arthur Marwick (The Nature of History). "The study spread over too long a period may seriously distort the objective reality of the past if it treats on the same footing material culled throughout the period on topics which may meantime have undergone significant change."

In addition to the above two methods of arrangement, there are other criterials which can also be adopted for the arrangement of historical material, *viz.*, geographical and other one based on personality. "Although geographic method may be an objective form of arrangement, but it is not constant" according to Louis Gottschalk (Understanding History). In short the best system of grouping the facts is to combine both chronological arrangement as well as the topical system.

(8) Exposition and Documentation

Exposition is the final part of the art or science of thesis preparation. In the narrative stage, it is fundamental to observe that sentences should be short, simple and declarative. As Heras points out, "the main principle to guide a researcher when beginning to write, after his materials have been collected, is that the historical narrative must be subjective, according to the reality of the happenings not according to the author's feelings. Bias should not find place in the historical writing as far as possible. Impartiality should be the guiding principle of any research scholar. Apart from these the research scholar or historian should possess the command of the languages in which he is writing. A forceful style is an essential factor in writing. But historical narrative should not be the servant of style. On the other hand style should be subordinated to historical narrative."

Elegant style consists in straight-forward presentation avoiding complex and compound sentences.

The language should be economical but rigorous. It should be clear and unambiguous.

The language should never be flowy or showy and figures of speech must be avoided. Even dullness is preferable to flambuoyancy.

The superlative must be kept to a minimum.

Praise and blame to other scholars shall find no place in a responsible thesis.

'Documentation' means the 'furnish of documents to substantiate a claim or some datum in the thesis; this may also be the means for refuting some one else's claim, if need be. Every important idea in the thesis is to be documented, it is not necessary to document all the well known statements.

This documentation shall be in the form of notes, appended at the foot of each page; the note for each point raised in the text must be typed at the foot of that page itself. Alternatively the notes can be given as reference at the end of each chapter, in which case they will be called references and not foot-notes.

Footnotes: The purpose of a footnote is twofold; 1. to indicate the source from where the idea or a quotation is taken. 2. to elaborate certain ideas which will be needed by the thesis for explanation but if included in the text will interfere with the easy flow of narration of the text. These can be in the form of short quotations or the scholar's comments. Very long quotations from original source are not desirable. If it run to many pages it would be better to quote only the most essential part of it.

The footnote citation is usually in the following order: author, title of publication, publisher and place of publication are essential only for the biographical entry but not for the footnote references.

The thesis must be typed on the right hand side only on demy size bond paper, leaving at least half an inch space on the right side to avoid typed matter being sliced off by the binder, and two inches on the left side for the typed matter to escape being hidden in the binding and one inch on top and one inch in the bottom leaving a space for 25 lines of typed matter normally per page

The typing should be double space for the text and single space for footnotes. The type should be neat and clean.

The footnote reference numbers must be given at the appropriate places, in the text as super numbers. The concerned footnotes should appear on the same page; and the footnotes must be serially numbered for each chapter each footnote must be started on a fresh line with its number preceding it. There should be no typographical errors. Any abbreviations used in the footnotes or the text should be standard and a list of abbreviations must be either prefixed or suffixed to the thesis.

Sample footnote entries :

(a) M. Arokiaswamy (1972), The Kongu Country, P .....

(b) M. Nanjundappa, The Guilds of Medieval Karnataka (A.D. 1000 —1500) (unpublished Ph. D. thesis, Mysore University, 1976), P....

(c) A.B. Keith, History of Sanskrit Literature, Oxford, 1928 p. 240.

Speech should always be put within double inverted commas, and mere words and phrases within single inverted commas, the dash should be sparingly used; too many dashes and parenthetical phrasing make reading very difficult for the peruser.

Numbering of Chapters and Pages: There should be an agreed system in the use of numerals. The Roman numerals *i.e.* I, II, III, IV etc., or i, ii, iii, iv etc., could be used for chapters and for paginating the pre-text material in the thesis, *i.e.*, from the title page to the beginning of the text. The text itself must be in Arabic numerals, as also the footnote reference numbering. All lists must be in Arabic numerals. In the contents, chapter numbers have to be in Roman numerals and the page numbers in Arabic numerals.

In using historical years the A.D. must precede the figure like A.D. 1789 and B.C. must follow the figure like 324 B.C.

Bibliography

The word 'Bibliography' is derived from the Greek word 'Biblio' which means 'book.' Any list of books can be called bibliography. In the broader sense bibliography is the science that deals with the history of books, their physical description, printing, publication, edition etc. It is the science of book referencing. In the stricter sense, a bibliography is a list of published works, although by common usage, both published and unpublished materials are listed in a bibliography. Information about books and other materials are found in it.

Bibliography of the list of books consulted by the researcher in the course of his research must be listed alphabetically otherwise; either exhaustive list of books on the subject or a select list actually consulted and used can be given. Books of a primary nature, of a secondary nature in different languages, encyclopaedias, journals, unpublished thesis, persons interviewed for oral history etc., are to be separately listed. Maps and charts, tables and illustrations can be either provided at proper places in the text or at the end of the thesis and placed before the bibliography.

Thus, a scientific method is an important aspect of historical investigation and research which must be followed by one and all. Heras observes thus: "A study on methodology will make it clear that historical work is not a work for all to take up. It requires a versatile mind, a special training, and a critical sense not possessed by the common run of men."

The following model should be observed:

Sample Title page of a Thesis. (See next page)

TITLE OF THE THESIS

A THESIS

Submitted in partial fulfilment of the
requirements for the degree of
Doctor of Philosophy
(in History)
in the University of ....

by

Name

Month and Year.

CERTIFICATE

This is to certify that the thesis "..................................." is based on the original work done by (Name) during (Years); and that this has not previously formed the basis for the award of any degree, diploma, associateship, fellowship or other similar title.

Signature of the Candidate
(Date)

Signature of the Supervisor
(Date)

Bibliography

(Sample notes taken on a slip from a book)

1.	KEITH, A.B.	*History of Sanskrit Literature,* (1928) pp. 240-241 (Hints to be given).
2.	Sample notes from a Journal entry RAJA VIDHYA	No. 1 April 1964, pp. 190-191 (Some points to be given).
3.	Foot note citation M. AROKIASWAMY	*The Kongu Country* (1972), pp. 50-55.
4.	Bibliographical entries NILAKANTA SASTRI, K.A.	*Sources of Indian History*, Bombay, 1964.
5.	Sample footnote entries R. CALDWELL.	*A Comparative Grammar of the Dravidian Languages*, 2nd ed. London, 1975, p. 64 ff.
6.	Chapter in a book with a single author N. SUBRAMANIAN	*The Hindu Tripod and other Essays: Caste in the Tamil country*, the author 1976, pp. 205.
7.	Epigraphic references: ARE 1921	Part II, Para 49.
8.	Sample Bibliographical entries SUBRAMANIAN, N.	*History of Tamilnadu* (to A.D. 1336) pp. 174-177.
9.	Multi-author publication MARSHALL, SIR J. and Others	*Indus Civilisation* (3 Vols.) London, 1931.
10.	Translated Work (Max Muller, F. [tr])	*The Upanishads*, 2 Vols., S.B.E. i xv, Oxford, 1879-82.
11.	Journal Article GEIGER (tr)	*Mahavamsa*, 2nd impression with addendum by G.C. Mendis Colombo, 1950.
12.	Abbreviations used E.I. Epigraphic Indica, J.I.H.	*Journal of Indian History.*

13.	Multivolume work with different editors and authors Various Authors.	*The Cambridge History of India* 6 Vols. (Vol. II not yet published) Cambridge 1972.
14.	A subsequent edition of a multi-author publication MAJUMDAR, R.C. and Others	*Advanced History of India*, (2nd ed.), London, 1950.
15.	Inscriptions KONOW STEN (ed.)	*Kharoshthi Inscriptions*, London, 1928.
16.	Government Records	Military Despatches from England Fort St. George Consultations.

Index

O

P

Q

R

S

T

U

V

W

X

Y

Z